FLYING by the SEAT of MY SOUL

Judith

Fly high!

Teri Marshall

10/18/03

FLYING by the SEAT of MY SOUL

Tess Marshall

Tess Marshall

Contact information:
Tess Marshall
688 Cascade West Parkway
Grand Rapids, MI 49546

Phone: 616-460-6729
Fax: 616-957-0249
Website: www.TessMarshall.com

Cover design: Gayle Raymer
Inside layout: Ad Graphics, Inc.

Printed in the United States of America

ISBN: 0-9742281-0-9

Acknowledgments

To all of those angels who have provided me the thrust needed to fly! Thank you!

Norm Jabin: For naming and advising me on my book!

Judy Smith: For your gentle nature, generous spirit and love that you have shared with my family.

Don Downer: For showing me how to serve others, teaching me tact, and believing I was college material.

Craig Bleckley: For sharing your math brain!

Wil VanderPol: For being my friend, mentor, and brave enough to tell it like it is! Marcia Maynard and Patti Felix: For unconditional acceptance, love and laughter.

Robert Temple: Blessings for your computer expertise, patience, and friendship.

Karen Fife: For your quiet support and teaching me to toot my own horn.

Pat MacEnulty: For "expert editing services."

To all the "happy learners," you know who you are.

My parents: Thank you both for the gift of life and so many brothers and sisters! My work is part of your legacy.

Kay Nuyens and Barb Badolati: For sharing and caring and traveling with me.

Connie Maitland: For being my friend through thick and thin.

Dana Ziebarth: For leading us to Torch Lake; your art has rocked my world.

Chris, Judy, Rose and Jan: For showing me that friends are for life.

To my clients: For your trust in me.

My children—Roshelle, Nicole, Kara, and Kristy: You have blessed my life beyond measure.

My grandchildren—Mackenzie, AJ and Ariel: You have offered me a love like no other. You fill me with joy from head to toe. I love you more!

And to the love of my life, Roger Marshall: You have walked by my side for 35 years. You have allowed me the freedom and the space I needed to grow inside and out. Thanks for believing in me, and listening to years of my dreams and goals. Thanks for a life time of support, for being the best dad in the world and for loving me. I love you, too!

Dedication

*I dedicate this book to the people
who have acknowledged that I've
made a difference in their lives.
Know that you've made a difference in mine.*

Contents

Preface

*"Do what you can,
with what you have, where you are."*
— Theodore Roosevelt

I spent the first 28 years of my life spiritually disconnected and flying by the seat of my pants. Pregnant at seventeen, I married my boyfriend, Roger. By the time I was 22, I had four little girls, the third pregnancy being twins. Roger had two jobs to support us, and desperate for extra income as well as an escape, I began a dried flower business. I felt overwhelmed, depressed, and inadequate as a mother and wife. I couldn't see the light at the end of tunnel. I felt I was off track in life and didn't know how to get back on. I was raised Catholic and attended parochial schools for eleven years. Yet as an adult, I felt spiritually disconnected. I felt a personal relationship with God was unattainable. Church on Sunday provided me with friends and peace and quiet for one hour. That is why I went.

My spiritual journey began after reading *Teach Only Love, That Is What You Are* by Jerry Jampolsky. For the first time I was introduced to a loving God. I released my fear of a "judgmental God in the sky that was going to get me some day" and began practicing living in a state of love and extending it to others. As I did something inside of me changed. My heart opened up to forgiveness, and I let go of past resentments. The first thing that changed was my relationship with my family. I trained my mind to be vigilant, witnessing the defenses of my ego and observing thoughts that were based in fear rather than love. I learned how to replace fear and judgment with thoughts of inner peace. I began to feel safe, loved and alive. I began to fly. I took the seat next to God as copilot and began flying by the seat of my soul.

Love, forgiveness, compassion and wisdom are experiences of the soul. Your soul is a positive force, spirit or energy at the core of your being. You are connected to God by your soul. Your soul is what allows you to see the good in everyone. Your soul only sees love. It is our personality or ego that distinguishes fat from skinny and rich from poor. Your soul sees the essence and value of each individual.

Soulful living is about inner wealth. It allows you to wake in glory each day with a heart filled with love. You are able to recognize how important your life is in the big scheme of things. Everything you do and say matters. It doesn't matter if you pick up garbage or do open heart surgery, you are contributing and adding meaning to our world. We are in this world together and share the responsibility of making it a brighter, more peaceful and loving place to be. In doing so we discover the meaning of life.

If we spend our lives doing the same things every day in the same manner, we will get the same results. If we want the world to be a better place, we need to participate in the transformation. I offer this book as a gift of hope to others who want to learn and grow. As you begin doing the soul stretching exercises at the end of each chapter, you will become open to God's guidance, presence and grace. Think of the exercises as flying lessons and begin to fly by the seat of your soul!

"Be glad of life! Because it gives you the chance to love and work, to play and to look up at the stars."

— Henry Van Dyke

Hitch Your Dream to a Star

"You have your colors, you have your brushes, paint paradise and walk right in."
— Nikos Kazantzakis

Are You Willing to Believe?

When we were growing up, didn't we believe that we could be anybody? If we let our imaginations run wild, a towel and a safety pin allowed us to become Superman. A new dress transformed us into dancing ballerinas, twirling to the point of exhaustion.

Today A.J., my grandson, puts on his Buzz Lightyear Halloween costume and runs through the house flying. My granddaughters Mackenzie and Ariel will put on my makeup and high-heeled shoes and become a fairy godmother and Cinderella. Their imagination allows them to dream they can be anybody. With their childlike spirit and imagination, they create their world.

When was the last time you allowed yourself to dream an impossible dream? What if you could do anything you wanted to do? Unlike children we often stop ourselves. We lack courage and faith. We allow our fears to stop us. Even if we find a mentor to help show us the way, we still have to do the work. Our dreams are connected to our purpose, our reason for being in the world. No one but you can fill your position. Nobody else has your vision, imagination, or insight. It is a big responsibility to live your purpose. Are you willing to do it?

When Mackenzie was seven years old, she was the only one in her second grade classroom who still had training wheels on her bike. One day my daughter took them off and told her she didn't have a choice; it was time to ride without them. Mackenzie was reluctant and frightened. My daughter and I took turns running beside her with words of encouragement, at the same time holding on to the back of her bike seat as she pedaled. It wasn't more than ten minutes, and she was off on her own. She spent the summer riding up and down the road not going very far. This year she rides her bike along side of her mom when she jogs, and she rides to her friend's house five blocks away. With a push and a guiding hand from those around her, Mackenzie gained independence and a whole new world to explore.

Often times I won't take action until I am backed in a corner and miserable. Like Mackenzie on her bike, I sometimes need a push in the right direction or someone to guide me. My first attempt at being a successful entrepreneur came out of desperation. When I was seventeen, I became pregnant and proceeded to have four children by the time I was twenty-two years old. Therefore, I needed work that I could do from home and on my own. I was juggling parenting and working for my father on the family farm when the opportunity arose.

On a beautiful summer day on my way home from working at the Muskegon Farmer's Market, I stopped off at Central Park in downtown Grand Haven. I had heard there was an art fair in the park. I discovered a middle-aged couple selling dried flowers that they had grown. Their booth was engulfed with women desperate to get a bouquet or an arrangement of just the right size and colors. As I watched with amazement and excitement, I knew immediately that I had the talent and passion to do what they were doing. It was what Oprah refers to as "a light bulb moment!"

My farming experience gave me the background I needed, and because I spent years out in nature and also helped my mom plant her flower gardens, I had developed an eye for color. After my insight at the park, I took action. I poured over my father's seed catalogs and found flowers called "Everlastings," which are grown specifically to dry so they last throughout the winter. I ordered the seeds and started with a small garden. I didn't doubt my abilities. I knew I was onto something big. When I want something bad enough, I will do almost anything to get it. I was a mover and a shaker without even knowing what that was. I was focused, determined, and what motivational speaker Les Brown calls "hungry." I was twenty-four and wanted an increased income to allow for more adventures and experiences for my kids. Roger already held two jobs to pay the bills. If I could figure out how to sell flowers like those people in the park were doing, we could afford to do more things. The first summer I sold my first bouquets in between my father's tomatoes and green beans. Over and over again, I went home with my basket empty and my pockets full.

I read every book I could find on dried flowers (there weren't very many at the time). My garden turned into two acres of land with irrigation pipe. I would weed, water, and harvest during the day with my children and make arrangements into the wee hours of the morning after putting them in bed at night. I ordered baskets, ribbon, and other supplies from a local wholesale house. That's when "Forever Flowers" was born.

As the business grew, I began training and paying my children to help me even more. Our weekends were spent at art fairs and summer festivals selling flowers. It was hard work, profitable, and fun at the same time. We met other artisans, and traded our flowers for jewelry, pottery, and hand-painted clothing. Food and entertainment were additional treats. I felt happy and alive, and my flowers helped others feel the same. Frederic Buechner has said, "God calls you at the place where your deepest gladness and the world's greatest hunger meet."

There were also challenges. We were dependent on the weather. Sometimes the flowers got too much rain and other times not enough. Sometimes we were rained out at the art fairs and our things were ruined. In every business there are challenges. Some you have control over and some you do not. You learn to do the best you can and surrender the rest. I was fortunate to have Roger who supported me. He also helped with the watering and the planting. He eventually traveled with us to help set up and tear down the booth and to load and unload vehicles. We went from packing and hauling our flowers in a station wagon to a van and finally a U-Haul truck as our business grew.

Eventually, we moved to the city and I began buying the flowers wholesale from other growers. For fifteen years we traveled all over Michigan and as far away as Chicago. All due to a young eager mother, who had faith in herself, had a light bulb moment, believed in her dream, gathered support, and acted upon it.

"I am capable of what every other human is capable of."

— Maya Angelou

Do You Have the Patience for Success?

I often assume that successful people "make it" over night. They either have more money than I or they know someone important and I do not. Sometimes this is true. Often, it is only my way of convincing myself of my inadequacy before I ever begin.

Rob Brown never studied acting and didn't have any professional acting experience. What he did have was a three-hundred dollar cell phone bill that needed to be paid. On a whim he auditioned for a part in a movie, was hired, and made his acting and motion picture debut as Jamal in *Finding Forester*. Call it a natural talent, a gift, Divine Order or a miracle. Success for most of us doesn't happen that quickly. It could, but most of us wouldn't allow it to happen that way. We stop ourselves without even trying. We rationalize in our minds why doing a spontaneous, brave act like this would be so ridiculous.

Every human being has a calling to be the best he or she can be. While most of us are called to become heroes in an ordinary life, some people have callings that require them to be famous and lose their anonymity. And the rest of us often worship famous people. It costs one hundred dollars per ticket to view Elvis Presley's mansion. It is important to put a star like Elvis in perspective. Elvis was a great singer, but I don't think he was successful. He died prematurely because of his addiction to drugs and alcohol. He lost control of his life and failed to connect his dreams to God. Admire the talent but don't worship the person. Remind yourself that you have gifts and talents as well. If you are using your talent, you can become an extraordinary person living an ordinary life.

Tiger Woods is successful not only because of natural talent but because of years of hard work, discipline, commitment, focus and undying, unshakable faith. Did you know that Tiger continues to get up at 5 a.m. on the morning of a tournament to practice his swing outside under special lighting? This is an example of tireless energy derived from living out a passion. Because he thinks success and acts successful, he becomes a magnet attracting even more success. He puts all of his energy and enthusiasm toward achieving his goal. In 1996 Tiger and his father Earl Woods began The Tiger Woods Foundation. It supports programs that focus on creating positive environments for underprivileged youths and that emphasize the importance of parental involvement and responsibility in the lives of children. Tiger is a modern day hero. His mind is centered in the realization that within him is the power to succeed.

Often we doubt our talent and ability to succeed. The question isn't whether you can be successful or not but are you willing to do what it takes to be successful? It is necessary to have the desire to make your dream come true. Allow it to become your reason for getting out of bed in the morning, the reason for burning the midnight oil. Believe in your dream and keep the faith. Pray for courage and strength to face your fears. Then hold a clear vision of yourself living your dream without any doubt.

When I began my private practice as a therapist, I had only a desk, a telephone and a telephone book. More importantly I had a zest for life, a desire for a new career and the enthusiasm to go for it. Samuel Goldwyn once remarked, "No person who is enthusiastic about her work has anything to fear from life." I began calling places that I believed would benefit from my services. I found a health club where I began doing workshops and seminars. I called the local paper and invited them to come and do a story. I was willing to do things I never did before.

Because of my willingness, passion and commitment, my practice continued to grow. If you do good work, your clients will recommend you to others. The place to begin is exactly where you are today. You create your success. You are responsible for where you are today and where you will be tomorrow. Be brave enough to leave your comfort zone and do what it takes to live your dream. Doors will open that you didn't even know were there.

Often we fail because we are impatient and want immediate gratification. Or we take giant steps instead of baby steps. Sometimes we beat ourselves up relentlessly for past errors we have made. In many cases we lose focus. We begin to doubt ourselves. We may feel that we can't reach our goals fast enough or we may feel left behind and left out. On difficult days we might want to give up completely.

I often see clients who have a desire to improve their health. They may eat less until the next dinner party or they might exercise more until the excitement from the new running shoes wears out. Eating healthy and exercising is for life! It is not something we hurry up and do before our next class reunion. If you want to change your eating or exercising habits, it is important to start out slow and make a commitment to a program that you can complete. Weight Watchers is successful because they have a plan that works. An important part of their plan is writing down every single thing you eat in a journal every day. That way you can't fool yourself.

Would you be willing to write in a journal? Breaking food addictions gives you more time and energy for your dreams. Ask yourself what type of exercise you prefer to do. Don't pay attention to the latest fad unless it fits your lifestyle. If you want to walk and don't have a partner, go to the recreation department in your town and ask if you can start a group for walkers. Exercise at the same time, and it will become a habit like brushing your teeth. It's more likely that you will stick to an exercise program if you do it at the same time everyday. Make a commitment and begin today; you will never regret it.

When the path we are on seems long and difficult and we notice that we are beginning to lose faith, it is important to sit back, breathe and recall past successes. We need to trust the process. Errors and difficulty are part of the process. They force us to stretch our soul. Know that we are bigger than our mistakes. I like the Ojibway saying, "Sometimes I go about with pity for myself, and all the while Great Winds are carrying me across the sky."

When my granddaughter broke her arm, she first had it in a sling until the swelling went down. A week later a cast was put on. We played with her, we read to her, we held her, but we couldn't rush the healing process. We didn't doubt that her arm was healing. We just knew it was. We trusted the process. A baby begins walking around the age of one. We don't worry how a baby will do it. We don't insist on knowing the exact date or in which room of the house the first step will be taken. We trust the process from crawling to standing to walking. It is an inner knowing. We don't give it a second thought.

---

*"The future belongs to those who believe
in the beauty of their dreams."*

— Eleanor Roosevelt

The Music of Your Soul

Paganini was an emerging violinist and composer in the 1800s. He dreamed of an audience in a packed opera house that would jump to their feet with an ovation. The evening came. It was his turn for a solo. He felt terror and sickness in his stomach as he began to draw his bow—he had grabbed the wrong violin. He heard a voice deep within that said, "Play with what you've got." So he did. He had faith that even with this instrument, something might happen that would create magic with the music. As Paganini gave all he had within himself, the audience rose to ovation after ovation. He said: "Before tonight, I always thought the music came from my violin. Tonight I realized the music comes from within me." We often believe that our miracle comes from the world. The only miracle that's real must come through us, from that place in us where the spirit of God lives. The music is within everyone.

However, others will often try to discourage us from hearing that music within. In 1883, an engineer, John Roebling, had the idea to build the Brooklyn Bridge. Other experts told him his idea was impossible. It couldn't be done. Washington, Roebling's son, also an engineer, helped his father design the plan and get financing from the bank. Next, they hired the crew and began to build the bridge that spans the river between Manhattan and Brooklyn.

After a few months, an accident occurred on-site. John was killed, and his son was severely injured. Brain damage left him unable to walk or talk. They were the only ones who knew the plan for the bridge. Because Washington Roebling still had a clear mind, he developed a communication code as he lay in his bed. He could move one finger. With that finger he tapped out the code on his wife's arm to communicate to her the plan so the engineers could continue building the bridge. Washington Roebling tapped his instructions with one finger for thirteen years until the Brooklyn Bridge, an engineering miracle, was finally completed! I remember this story every time I want to give up when the going gets tough. I have repeated this story to my children, to clients, and to audiences, and it has never failed to inspire.

A more recent success story belongs to Wendy Kopp. In 1989, Kopp took note of the glaring inequality of education among socioeconomic levels of society. With her youthful energy and perspective, she used her senior thesis at Princeton University to propose the creation of Teach For America. TFA is a national corps of outstanding college graduates who pledge two years to teach disadvantaged students in some of the most under-served public schools across the country. Now in its thirteenth year, the organization has placed more than 7,000 dedicated corps members in urban and rural areas in an attempt to compensate for shortcomings in the public education system. The education disparity that Kopp originally sought to change still exists, but there is no doubt her organization makes a difference. Wendy and the corps members continue to leave a lasting impact on society. Because of her efforts and dedication, Wendy has received the Woodrow Wilson Award, the highest honor Princeton University confers on undergraduate alumni. I know this story well. My daughter Kristy is a past member of the corps.

Tiger Woods has set new standards for the game of golf. He is young and respected by his peers. He has won three master championships. He is changing the history of golf. He began as a young child, watching his father practice his swing from his high chair. His mother had a vision that he would be famous someday and saved the chair. It has taken him his whole life to get where he is today.

There are endless stories about people who refuse to give up. Read about them, learn from them and join them in living life to the fullest. When we are ready to commit to our dreams, nothing can stop us. If we start where we are, consistently taking baby steps even when we are frightened, we will succeed. When fear threatens to stop you, keep moving forward. Baby steps are better than no steps at all!

*"If one advances confidently in the direction of his dreams,
and endeavors to live the life which he has imagined,
he will meet with a success unexpected in common hours."*
— Henry David Thoreau

Soul Stretching

☆ ☆ ☆ ☆ ☆

1. Close your eyes and imagine yourself as an innocent child. What do you see? Do you see someone who loves life and has great expectations for life? Do you believe that anything is possible? With pen and paper begin a dialogue about possibilities and dreams with your inner child. With your dominant hand, write down a question (i.e. What do I need to feel safe? What is my next step?). Answer the question with your non-dominant hand. Put a picture of yourself at three years old in a frame and commit to believing in possibilities.

2. Create a Plan. Write your goals down. Read them every day. List at least three things you can do each morning that will move you towards your goals.

3. Write down your past successes, big or small. Write down your strengths.

4. List potential obstacles and write a plan to overcome each one. Are you willing to do what it takes?

5. Read, listen and affirm. Read a daily meditation book, a Bible, or inspirational stories. Listen to inspirational speakers who have overcome great obstacles. Write out affirmations and post them where you will read them daily.

6. Explore community education classes, job sections of the newspaper, and the internet in search of what might interest you. Ask yourself, if I could have any of those opportunities, which one would I choose? If I believed in myself, what would I begin today?

7. Inquire. Ask! Ask! Ask! Invite yourself into businesses that have what you are looking for. Find out who knows what and who knows whom. Be persistent!

8. Don't forget to ask for guidance, use your intuition and listen. We have all been blessed with many gifts and talents. Today is the best day to look within and see what is there or what has been hidden for a long time. Bring that talent, gift or opportunity into the light and dare to use it.

9. Make a list of 100 things you want to do in your lifetime. Date each item on your list as you accomplish each one. Keep this list ongoing.

10. Make a joy and excitement journal. Write down where you find excitement and joy in your life. Pay attention to that. Write down the details of a good day. This will help you connect to the desires in your heart.

"I am looking for a lot of men who have an infinite capacity to not know what can't be done."

— Henry Ford

Claiming Your Creativity

"Wherever you are is the starting point."
— Kabir

The Starting Point

We are born to create. Everyone is creative. One of my hobbies is painting on furniture. I love garage sales, flea markets and thrift stores. I look for unusual pieces that I can restore to life. In June I have a sale in my front yard. The month before the sale every room in my house is cluttered with chairs, tables, shelves and stools ready to be tagged for the sale. Often times there is paint on my phone, clothes, and floor. I don't care. My best work comes from this mess. Granddaughter Mackenzie sorts and prices her old toys and puts up the card table herself. It gives me such joy to watch her become animated and talkative. At the end of one sale, I noticed everything left on her table was marked nine dollars! She probably saw that number on one of my items and copied it. My daughter and I laughed ourselves silly at the sweetness and joy of it all. The following year my granddaughter Ariel came with her toys and joined in the fun!

My daughter Shelly takes great delight in my creativity. She watches and admires everything I do. One time she waited for me to get home from work so I could make the Indian corn decoration for her front door. She could have done this herself, but she preferred to have me do it. Later, when it came to painting, Shelly again wanted me to do it for her rather than learn how to do it herself. By refusing to do so, I convinced her to try. I helped her choose colors and brushes, showed her some methods and left her on her own. That is what a good teacher does. We are often tempted to hover over, making sure it is done the correct way or our way! It is not from our knowledge or instruction that our students learn. It is in the creating itself. When it comes to creativity, there is no right or wrong. Creativity just is! Because I left Shelly alone and because I refused to do it for her—she now paints! She painted her wicker furniture periwinkle. Her bathroom cabinets are purple. She painted all kinds of flowerpots. Her kitchen is blue, and Mackenzie's chest of drawers is yellow with blue polka dots.

Three things happened. I didn't do it for her. I encouraged her. I told her if you don't like it or it doesn't turn out, PAINT OVER IT! There are no mistakes, just pure energy that we call creativity waiting to be released.

As adults our creativity is either hidden or blocked. We are socialized out of it at an early age. When my grandson AJ hears music playing, he will begin dancing immediately. His smile becomes a mile wide! He is free and full of energy. My granddaughters love to cut, glue and paste. They don't want directions—only the tools and freedom to explore on their own. They also love to sing. If you call their home the phone recording is of them singing, "Hello, Hello, Hello, and how are you? I'm fine. I'm fine. I hope that you are, too." Creativity in a child is expressed when a box becomes a train car, a pile of sand becomes a castle or a colored picture becomes a precious gift. You can bet five years from now there will not be a singing message on the recorder, their dancing will become awkward and artwork on the refrigerator will be replaced with basketball, football and soccer schedules. Like us they will become embarrassed and shamed right out of their drawing, singing and dancing. As children we are socially conditioned out of our creativity. It becomes compartmentalized. As adults it is necessary to remove the blocks that keep us from expressing it or denying that it exists at all. If creativity isn't allowed to resurface in your work and play, life becomes stale and stagnant, you become the living dead.

The next time you hear your favorite song on the radio, sing along! Dance in your living room and invite a three-year-old over to paint or draw. (By age five they have already learned not to go outside the lines!) There is risk involved in unblocking your creativity. You have to let go of perfection and judgment. Creativity is often blocked by fear because the outcome is uncertain. Our fear keeps us stuck in our office, often times in work we don't enjoy, with books in alphabetical order, papers neatly filed away and an emptiness that we feel in every cell of our body. Life doesn't change until you risk stepping out of your routine and order and into the unknown.

Creativity comes from trust. Learn to trust the process. I often tell clients that no one is grading you! There is no perfection. There is nothing to fear. Give yourself permission to be a beginner. When you unleash your creativity, a whole new world will lie at your feet. The sun becomes brighter and the birds sing louder. Like a child running free at recess, you laugh, run, and explore thrilled to be alive. You can feel your blood pulsating in your body, and your heart beats to the tempo of nature. Beautiful as a butterfly, you flit from one activity to another leaving your unique stamp on everything you touch.

We often think that best-selling books are written over night. Looking at it that way gives us an excuse not to pick up a pencil. If you want to be an author, write every day. That's what authors do. If you want to paint or draw, set aside time daily to do it and your artwork will improve. That's what artists do. If you want to be a speaker, get out and speak in your community, never turn down a speaking opportunity. That's what speakers do.

What if we put as much time into our creativity as we do other things? What if we had a journal or sketchbook in every bedroom instead of a television? What if we carried around our pen and notebook or paintbrush and easel like we do our cell phones? Too often we want to be good immediately. Discovering and unblocking our creativity takes time. Articles, newsletters and books take patience, editing, courage and commitment. When is the last time you allowed yourself to believe in impossible things? In the book *Through The Looking Glass* by Lewis Carroll, the Queen tells Alice she believed as many as six impossible things before breakfast. If you believed in six impossible things before breakfast what would they be? Open your journal and make a list.

"It is through creating, not possessing, that life is revealed."
— Vida D. Scudder

What Are You Willing to Do Differently?

Roger and I celebrated our thirtieth wedding anniversary in Hawaii. On the island of Oahu, we hiked through a bamboo forest. We discovered that when a bamboo seed falls to the ground, it is watered and nourished by the rains and nutrients in the soil. During the first year nothing happens. During the second and third years, the rains and soil feed the bamboo seed again and nothing happens. During the fourth year, the pattern continues and nothing happens. Suddenly, in the fifth year, during a span of less than six weeks, the bamboo grows ninety feet. Did the bamboo grow to be ninety feet in six weeks or five years? To the untrained eye, it appears as if nothing happened during the first four years. Nature teaches patience. The bamboo grows ninety feet in five years. If nature gave up on the bamboo, it would die. It is important to resist the temptation to give up on your dream before reaching your destination.

An American woman named Joan was visiting the French resort town of Nice. One day at an open-air market, Joan saw the great painter and her idol, Pablo Picasso. She approached him and explained that she was one of his biggest fans. She asked him if he would mind doing a quick sketch of her and offered to pay him. Picasso studied the woman for a few seconds, picked up his sketchpad and charcoal and began. Fifteen minutes later he handed Joan the finished portrait. Joan loved it, and couldn't thank the artist enough. Joan took out her checkbook and asked how much she owed. Picasso answered 5,000 francs. Joan protested, "But it only took you fifteen minutes to do the drawing."

The master replied, "You don't understand. It took me eighty years and 15 minutes to draw."

How much time are you willing to spend to unblock your creativity? What are you willing to do different? What could you explore with unleashed creativity? Leave your comfort zone. Is there a book inside of you? Is there a project you have always wanted to tackle but didn't have the courage? What gifts and talents do you have that terrify you? Don't take them to the grave with you. Leave a legacy, a mark on the world that only you can make.

I often do crafts with my grandchildren. It is their favorite thing to do. Our favorite activities are painting and putting on puppet shows. One of Mackenzie's projects at school this year was to paint her favorite storybook on a t-shirt. She painted the title of the book on the front of the shirt and Amelia Bedelia doing something silly on the back along with her favorite paragraph. Wearing their masterpieces the school children paraded through the other classrooms. Later the teacher hung their shirts on a clothesline for display. It was all part of learning to love to read. Mackenzie is so proud to be a "reader."

How can you be more creative in your work? What are you willing to do differently? What risk would you be willing to take? Go ahead and dare to mess up your project. Don't let the new piece of paper intimidate you.

Julia Cameron, author of *The Artist's Way*, asks us to write three pages every morning. She calls it brain drain. Would you be willing to do that? I have led groups using her book several times. I have seen members try new hobbies and others change careers. A yoga, drawing or dance class could be the feast that your soul has been starving for. How could you become more conscious and creative in your everyday living?

As for me, Sunday I am going to paint, Wednesday my creative friends are coming over so we can offer each other support in our life work, and Friday I am going to pick up my grandchildren and exhaust myself with silly play.

"My future starts when I wake up every morning ...
every day I find something creative to do with my life."
— Unknown

What Inspires You?

I attribute my endless creativity to the life I led working on the family farm. I was born into it. My sisters and I worked out in the fields in the sun, in the cold, in the rain and in the midst of lightning and thunder. We were always planting, weeding, picking, and playing on my family's 88-acre produce and trucking farm. There we chased our shadows and basked in nature and all of its glory season after season. The contrast of the glorious colors of the sky, the earth and the fruits and vegetables were breathtaking.

We did the most difficult jobs in the morning before the sun would get the best of our energy. We often came upon intricate spider webs shining with morning dew. Tons of strawberries, pickles, melons and green and yellow beans would be picked, packed, and loaded on refrigerated trucks for the following day at the Farmer's Market. I can still taste the tomatoes we would pick and eat from the vine while we worked. They were red, ripe, sweet, and warm from the mid-day sun.

Picking melons was one of my favorite jobs. It wasn't back breaking. We would crack open watermelons on the ground and eat the heart out with our hands. The juice would drip down our chins and our arms as we devoured the sweet seedless part. As we worked our way from one field to the next, I couldn't help but notice that the texture of the brown, sandy high ground compared to the black, mucky low ground was as different as night and day. During the summer, we would catch pollywogs, swim and fish in the pond. All of my senses were heightened by these experiences.

Gladiolas are often used at funerals, but to me they hold memories of happy creative times with my sisters. In the late afternoon the gladiolas seemed to stand in the fields at attention proud and arrayed in shining glory as if they couldn't wait for us to take them from the field and send them on their way to brighten somebody's day, true to their purpose. We always "bunched" in the evening. "Six in a bunch," my father would yell to us over the blaring radio as we chatted and filled the empty buckets with water. He left it totally up to us to mix or match the colors. He trusted us to use our intuition. It was one of our favorite times of the day.

My sister Jan loved these flowers enough to choose white ones to decorate the church at her September wedding. Each one of her bridesmaids wore a different color dress and each carried a matching color of gladiolas in her bouquet. I was in seventh grade and wanted so badly to be included in her wedding that she allowed me to be her junior bridesmaid. I wore an orange taffeta dress and carried a bouquet of orange-gold gladiolas. It was one of the first times I remember feeling important. That doesn't happen very often when you are one of ten children.

In the early evenings, we would all go out after dinner to dig the potatoes. My brother Stan would drive the tractor that pulled the potato digger. It would throw the plants above the ground, and then two of my younger siblings would shake the plants until the potatoes fell loose. Then the rest of us would pick them up two by two carrying the crates between us. Silently, I looked in awe at those green plants and red and white potatoes lying on top of the rich sandy soil. I remember the distinct smell of the evening air, the dirt and the new potatoes.

At the farmer's market, we learned how to display the produce to appeal to the customers. The green and yellow beans would be dumped by the bushels next to the neatly arranged red ripe tomatoes. Next to the red peppers would be the yellow summer squash and zucchini. Contrasting those would be sweet white onions, pickles and the buckets of flowers. The cantaloupe and watermelons would always be side by side with plates of sweet mouth-watering samples.

It was a sensory experience growing up on the farm. The smells, the tastes, the sights and the sounds are embedded in my memory. Often today the explosive squish of a cherry tomato in my mouth or eating hot buttered corn and acorn squash filled with brown sugar trigger sweet memories of the foods I ate as a child. My mother lined our pantry with shelves of canned tomatoes, dill pickles, and raspberry, peach and strawberry jams. I go back in time every time I see a flower growing or a bee buzzing. So when someone tells me I have an "eye" for color, I smile and say, "The farm." In itself it was a living, vibrant palette. Escaping in the vast beauty of our natural workplace was how we survived the endless workdays of summer.

Creativity is innate. Our lives and our experiences are created anew each day with our thoughts, words, and actions. Tomorrow doesn't have to be the same as yesterday. Find some small way to be creative today:

- Try a new restaurant or at least a new item on the menu.

- Ride your bike or walk to work one day a week.

- Rearrange the furniture in your home or office.

- Wear an unusual color.

- Paint your kitchen a bright new color.

- Change your perfume or cologne.

- Learn something that you know nothing about.

- Subscribe to a new magazine.

- Take the stairs instead of the elevator.

- Park your car in a different place.

- Go to the zoo and focus on the color of the animals.

These small changes will open the way for new creative juices to flow. We have the opportunity to create happy and fulfilling lives. Begin today to allow your creative juices to color a whole new world!

Soul Stretching

☆ ☆ ☆ ☆ ☆

1. Take yourself on a play date: Go to your local craft store and buy artist supplies—paint, paper, pencils, unfinished wood, etc. Store them in a special place to be used as a creative break.

2. Write: You will need a quiet place, a pencil or pen and paper. Commit to writing in this space for a half hour, three times per week. That is all you need to get started. Once you commit to doing this, you will find yourself writing for longer periods of time. Choose any topic or object as your subject. Look at old photographs and write their stories.

3. Music: Listen to music that you liked as a child. Listen to classical, rock, and jazz. Expand your knowledge of music. You might even find an opportunity to join a choir or play that instrument you always wanted to play but never had the opportunity.

4. Nature Walks: Take walks in different kinds of weather. Notice how you feel. Notice how many pine needles are on a branch or the texture of the bark of a tree. Look at an object for ten minutes. Write in your journal what you observe: the color, smell or size. Sketch the object. What memories come up for you? What did Walt Whitman mean when he said, "With every leaf a miracle…?"

5. Spend time with children. Laugh when they laugh. Look when they look. Pretend when they pretend. Allow them to lead you. Learn from them how to greet the world with wide-eyed wonder.

6. Complete the following sentences:

   This year I want to be . . .

   This year I want to do . . .

   This year I want to have . . .

   This year I want to go . . .

   This year I want to see . . .

   My intention is to . . .

7. Soul time: Each year take time to spend a long weekend or more to be with yourself in solitude. Ideas multiply when you take the opportunity to reflect on your soul's calling. A few times a year, I go to our cottage to spend time alone. It is wonderful to be with the lake, woods, and fresh air as I reflect on my life. I read and write. I call this my "soul time." I return renewed, happy, and more connected.

8. Enroll in a class and learn something new. What would your life look like if you learned a new language, yoga, woodcarving or how to ski?

9. Plan to travel to a new place regularly. It could be to a different city or a different country. Experience a new restaurant, a new museum or a new path to hike.

10. Eliminate the word "can't."

"Make visible what, without you,
might perhaps never have been seen."

— Robert Bresson

Embracing Fear

It is not our fears that hold us back.
It is our belief that we are powerful beyond measure.
It is our light not our darkness that we fear the most.
We sometimes ask who am I to be brilliant,
magnificent, talented and gorgeous?
Actually who are you not to be?
You are a child of God.
Your playing small does not serve the world.
There is nothing enlightened about shrinking so
those around you won't feel insecure.
We are meant to shine like children do.
We were born to make manifest the
glory of God that is within us.
It is not in some of us. It's in everyone.
When we let our light shine, we unconsciously
give others permission to do the same.
When we are liberated from our fears our presence
automatically liberates others from theirs.
— Marianne Williamson

What Are You Afraid Of?

When is the first time you remember being afraid? Was it when you were very young? Perhaps it was as a baby alone in your crib and your mother walked out of the room? Or the day you entered kindergarten, or when you were knee high to adults and lost sight of a parent at a grocery store. As small children we usually panic and scream out in terror at the top of our lungs until someone familiar rescues us. As a frightened adult you might want to screech in terror again. Go ahead and do that in a place where no one will hear you. It will diffuse the fear and bring enough relief to nudge or push you to move forward.

Fear has a purpose; it keeps you from doing crazy things and prevents you from acting irrationally. Fear gives you time to think before you act. Being in touch with your fears is part of being in touch with who you are. It is healthy to admit that you are afraid, worried or anxious. To do so requires strength. There are times when you will want and need support. Ask for it. When you express worries and anxieties, they lose their power. When you are honest and open with a friend, lover or therapist, the rewards are often encouragement, comfort and even intimacy. You will never get rid of fear. You have two choices. You can obsess about your fears and allow them to stop you from taking action or you can starve them with trust and prayer.

We are all afraid. We are afraid of getting too close to others and losing them. We are afraid that we will hurt someone or someone will hurt us. We are afraid of not knowing anything and knowing too much. We fear losing control and being too controlling. We fear that good things won't happen and bad things will. We are afraid of being alone and not being alone enough. We are afraid of who we are and afraid of who we could be. We fear change and we fear not changing. We fear what we know and we fear the unknown. We fear failing and we fear succeeding. If you lack trust or feel dismay or dread, you are afraid.

These are universal fears. If we are going to live up to our full potential and fulfill our life purpose, we have no choice but to work through them. We do not reach our potential by playing it safe. If you are alive, you have fears. It is what you do with them and how you handle them that makes all the difference in the world. When you are afraid to take action, ask yourself, "Who will do this if I don't?"

If you look at the "turning points" in your life, you'll see that they are usually preceded by fears. Turning points are decisions you have made in the past that made a significant difference in your life. If you were to reflect on and list the accomplishments in your life, you could also reflect on and name your fears that you had prior to them.

When my twin daughters were four years old, they left for kindergarten; I left for Grand Valley State College (now a university) at the same time. I was 27 years old and terrified. I knew I was smart but I had not done well in school. On the farm our studies were not a priority, work was. There was never time allowed for studying until the work was finished. The problem was it was never finished. The better we did with one crop the more my father would have us plant the next time. We were always planting extra this and extra that. In the fall we would pick the late crop of string beans after school. I remember picking in the rain, our backs aching, our fingers freezing and so numb I couldn't feel the beans. I just looked and grabbed. We weren't allowed to quit until they were all picked. Consequently, we were too tired to study, so when it came to grades my siblings and I all slid by.

In the first semester of my sophomore year of high school, I failed Spanish. If you have ever taken a language class, you know that you have to retain what you learn. I didn't. And I didn't have the time to review. I was in big trouble with my father. Maybe giving us the time to study wasn't a priority, but he expected us to do well anyway. When we did get bad grades, we were punished. In order to avoid punishment, I learned how to cheat. I just didn't see any other choice. Passing algebra was a graduation requirement. So a few of my friends and I would meet in the cafeteria. My best friend, Kathy, was the one in our group who mastered numbers. The rest of us all copied her work first thing in the morning. We were only caught once. My final grade was a C. I never took another math class in high school. My fear growing up was that I was incapable and stupid.

It was a priest from the local Catholic Church who convinced me to go to college. I was afraid I wasn't smart enough, but he wouldn't take no for an answer. He helped me choose two classes, "How to Study" and "Speed Reading." He understood my fears and showed me around campus pointing out the buildings where my classes were held. That first semester I did well in both of my classes. Father Don was a pivotal person in my life, and attending college was a turning point.

Because being a good parent was my priority, I never carried more than two or three classes at a time. When it came time to take college algebra, I knew I was in trouble. In order to get into the class, I took basic math and pre-algebra which required extra money and earned credits that wouldn't count towards my degree. My mind was made up; I would do whatever it took to graduate. The first day of algebra class, my mouth was dry, my heart pounding with a firm belief that I wouldn't be able to understand. I was afraid I wasn't smart enough or deserving enough or good enough. Instead of giving in to my fears, I found the tutoring center and scheduled appointments twice a week.

I also had the help of my friend Craig, who was the local high school math teacher. I asked him for a textbook which had the answers in the back. That way when I worked on problems late at night after the children were sleeping, I was able to find out immediately if I was solving the problems correctly. He also reassured me that I could call him for help even in the middle of the night. Craig taught me to look at the story problems as puzzles. He never doubted I could do them.

On the day of the final exam, an enormous amount of crumpled papers littered my study area. I felt confident, but at the same time I was worried I wouldn't get all the problems finished within the time limit. I remember leaving the building when the exam was finished. My shoulders and neck ached from tension. I grabbed my gym bag and went to the track and ran five miles. Then I went home and made dinner because the girls would be dropped off soon from the school bus. I passed the class with a C+. I could have whined and complained about a low grade after all the extra effort, but I didn't. I happily took my grade, patted myself on the back and signed up for more classes.

Nine years after those first two classes, I graduated. Roger, my mom and the kids were cheering and waving loudly as I walked across that stage to accept my diploma. I was elated! Taking Don's advice and entering college was a "turning point" in my life. Hemingway wrote, "The world breaks everyone and afterward many are strong at the broken places." I felt strong, able and ready to conquer the world that day! Too many people give up when things become difficult. They would rather give up their dream than risk failure. If you follow your heart, people will be put on your path to help you. They will appear in unexpected, unpredicted, and even magical ways.

When I finished my bachelor's degree, I knew that I wanted to get a Master's in Psychology. I found myself trembling once more because of the writing it would require. I asked my friend Will, a practicing psychologist, if he would mentor me. Again I doubted my capability. I was uncertain that anyone would hire me. I had heard that there was an overabundance of therapists and not enough clients to go around. I had heard that insurance companies were no longer covering therapy and HMO's had closed their panels and new therapists would not be allowed to be providers. Unlike the many years it took to complete my undergraduate work, I finished my Master's Degree in two and a half years with a Specialty in Alcohol and Substance Abuse. And I discovered that there will always be a need for helping professionals and that it is never too late to manifest your genius.

Whatever it is you wish to do, the power is in you to do it. Once you discover your passion, you can realize your dreams. If you can learn to commit to the work, trust the process, and live in the moment, God will take care of the details.

However, you will not be able to live your dreams without first confronting fears. My friend Patti once told me that God will get you through anything but out of nothing. So ask your Higher Power for the help and trust you need. Your talents are unique; no one can do your life work the way you can. There is only one Oprah and there is only one YOU! If you are meant to be a teacher, the universe will provide the students. If you are meant to be a doctor, God will provide the patients. Without knowing the outcome, it is necessary to begin. Every dream begins with taking the first step, then the second, and the third. The problem is you think you need to know HOW it will happen. You think you need to see the whole picture. What you want is control! What you want is a guarantee, and life doesn't come with guarantees.

When I was young, we had neighbors who owned horses. Sometimes after the work was finished, we would be allowed to go over and ride them. One day while galloping back to the barn, I fell off the horse. David, the horse's owner, was right behind me. After seeing that I wasn't hurt, he insisted I immediately get back on the horse and continue. I finished the ride. Why did David want to put me back on the horse so soon? So I wouldn't have time to think myself into the fear that would prevent me from riding again. The minute I was back on the horse, I saw it was an isolated incident. When you are afraid, you need courage and faith; combined with action you have what it takes to move mountains.

> *"To keep our faces toward change and behave like free spirits in the presence of fate is strength undefeatable."*
>
> — Helen Keller

Allow Nothing to Stand in Your Way

Paul Orfalea flunked second grade. He had difficulty reading and writing. His parents found it necessary to hire tutors and put him in special classes. During his school years, he lived with humiliation and low self-esteem.

Paul eventually learned that he had dyslexia. It didn't stop him from graduating from community college with a B average. He then entered the University of Southern California. Paul was part of a study group there working on a project when he made a deal with his classmates. Because he couldn't read well, he offered to be the 'gofer' if the others wrote the paper. They agreed.

In the 1970's the copy machine was still new. While making copies for his study group he became fascinated with it. He had the insight to know photocopying was going to change the way we reproduced documents in the future.

Paul borrowed five thousand dollars from the bank, rented a space near the university and began a photocopy shop. The shop didn't require much inventory. He charged four cents a page for copies. The campus library was charging ten cents. As his little business boomed, he decided to sell school supplies to students. He strapped backpacks on some of the male students and sent them to the women's dorms to take orders. Then he sent female students to do the same in the men's dorms. Paul took on his friend, Brad Kraus, as a business partner who began a second store. Twenty-six years and 127 partnerships later, Kinko's had almost 1,000 stores. Paul is a no excuse man. He didn't use dyslexia as an excuse to prevent him from being successful.

"The creative is the place where no one else has ever been. You have to leave the city of your comfort and go into the wilderness of your intuition."

— Alan Alda

Are You Willing to Leave Your Comfort Zone?

You can't go beyond your fear without leaving your comfort zone. It is easy to cling to comfort even if it is painful. Often in my practice I see single people who fear that if they leave their present miserable relationships they are doomed to live a life alone. For example, Bob is in an abusive relationship with his partner of three years. Sue has been married three times prior to living with Bob. Recently Sue has admitted to having an affair. Bob is devastated but claims that they have great sex and the chemistry is right. He can't imagine a life without Sue. Bob doesn't want to be alone, and he doesn't believe there is another woman for him. Bob is going to stay with Sue and choose to live a comfortable and familiar life of pain.

Of course, there is no guarantee that there will be somebody else. Not knowing what lies ahead, not having faith that there is someone better keeps Bob stuck in a life of painful abuse. It keeps him immobilized, even when he knows in his heart he deserves a faithful partner. Choosing a life of misery is familiar and risk free. Choosing to trust in a brighter future is fearful. Bob would rather live in an abusive relationship than take the risk of living alone and possibly find someone who will respect, honor and treasure him.

Not only do people sometimes get stuck in unhealthy relationships, some people also stay in dead end jobs because they are too afraid to leave. Some stay because they have good benefits. Others stay because they need the money to keep up their current lifestyle. It takes faith to change jobs. It takes faith to live on less. It takes faith to learn new skills or take a class to further your career. Ruts are familiar and feel safe.

The trapeze acts at the circus always amazed and intrigued me when I was a little girl. There are a few moments when one lets go of one bar before catching the next. The person is literally in mid-air for a few seconds hanging on to nothing. Those are the moments you fear the most. The moments you have nothing to hang on to. Yet if you don't let go of one bar you will never catch the second.

Several years ago a job requirement of mine was to counsel prisoners. I was told that it would be group therapy. On my first day I was terrified. I was literally shaking in my shoes. A probation officer led me to the room where we would work. I was shocked to see 23 prisoners staring back at me. Anyone whose crime was related to drugs and alcohol was required to be there. This was their idea of group therapy! An ideal group for therapy is about seven people. So I took on the role of a teacher instead of a therapist.

Often I would begin by reading a story from *Chicken Soup for the Soul*. Through these readings and our discussions, they learned how to overcome obstacles, about the rewards of forgiveness, and about the miracle of love. Eventually my knees stopped shaking, and I realized I had a captive audience! We talked about life values and how to get a G.E.D. I listened as they told me about their families, their kids, and the grandmothers they adored. I talked about how to stay sober and the rewards of a job that paid minimum wage when they could make a thousand dollars and more per day dealing drugs. Most of the people in that room preferred to be somewhere else. That didn't stop me from trying to reach them. Every Tuesday evening and Wednesday morning for one year, I literally walked through my fears by walking into prison. I believed if I could help one person stay sober, it would be worthwhile. That is when I realized if I could do this job, I could do anything! I figured they were a tough audience, and I survived. That experience jump-started my private practice and speaking profession.

My friend Laura has always wanted to live in a warmer climate. Michigan's winters are dark, cold and gray. Soon after Laura's daughter graduated from high school, she and her husband, Tom, decided it was time to go. Tom quit his job and left with a couple of leads for a new position. Laura, a spiritual counselor, would have to establish herself and find clients all over again once they settled into their new home. They would be strangers in a strange land. My friends do not give up easily. Their gratitude, trust and faith are a tremendous source of strength. Laura and Tom are risk takers. They suck the marrow out of life. It was not easy to make a move that would take them across country away from friends and relatives. But their happiness depended on it. They wouldn't be true to themselves had they remained.

Now, they live a block from the ocean. Was the move difficult? Yes. In the beginning, there were moments when they regretted moving. But a year later, they had new friends and plenty of work.

Do you find yourself worrying about the future of your job, the future of your children and grandchildren, and the future of the world? On September 11, 2001, we were jolted out of our comfort zones by terrorism. We have increased anxiety over flying, unemployment, the stock market and war. If you struggled with anxiety or depression previous to the attack on the World Trade Center, it is likely that it has increased. If you have lost your job, you may lack purpose. You might feel sad and confused one day and indifferent or angry the next. It is important to allow yourself to feel your emotions and get help and support if necessary.

Many times in my life, I have felt that things were out of control. I have struggled in the past with my family of origin, marriage, children, friends, addictions, employment, education, and to-do-lists. I have struggled with lack of faith, impatience, materialism, ego and apathy. I believe that all of the lessons I have learned from my past struggles and tumultuous times have given me the strength and courage I have today.

Author Dr. Christiane Northrup, says that when you feel equal amounts of exhilaration and terror, you are exactly where you need to be. The best advice in the world is to keep your attention on what is going right in your life and the joy of living. As Thoreau observed, too many people are living lives of quiet desperation. When you take the time to recognize your gifts and blessings, it is easier to keep going when life becomes difficult. Focus on what is going right in your life. Then stand tall and strong like a lighthouse and shine your love and light, so others can also find their way. Be committed to expressing your greatness.

Soul Stretching

☆ ☆ ☆ ☆ ☆

1. Talk to God. Invite God to be your friend. Take God with you wherever you go. Into a board meeting: "God, what do you think of these ideas?" Into the morning rush hour: "God, should I allow that person to cut in front of me?" Into your home: "God, do we spend enough time with each other?" If you want to have peaceful day, include conversation with God. Remind yourself that God is always with you.

2. Lighten up and laugh. Laughter is an enemy of depression, fear, and anger. You can tell the health of a family or workplace by how much laughter you hear. Let go of life being perfect and going smoothly. Learn to roll with the punches. Read the cartoons and watch comedy.

3. Make a list of everything you have succeeded at in your life. Place the list where you can see it for the times you doubt yourself.

4. Draw or paint your fear. Dialogue with your fear. Ask with your dominant hand—Fear, what are you here to teach me? Write your answer with your non-dominant hand. Continue dialoguing until you feel at peace.

5. Listen to Music. Music is healing. Classical music can reduce stress. Rock and Roll can give you energy. Chanting can bring you into a meditative state. Children's music can make your heart smile. Johann Paul Friedrich Richter said, "Music is the moonlight in the gloomy night of life." Listening to music that you like will increase inner peace.

6. Live the next seven days without fear. When a fear comes up, jot it down in a notebook and tell the fear you will get back to it later.

7. Know that you are part of God's healing plan. Your participation is needed. Fear is not part of God's plan for us, love is. So get going and do your part. The world needs you now more than ever!

8. Reach out and trust someone. Tell them your fears and ask for their support.

9. Realize that happiness is internal; it is a feeling in your heart. Begin the practice of placing your hand on your heart and asking, "How does my heart feel today?" If there is fear in your heart, remember you can replace it with a memory of a happy time.

10. Only a little faith is needed to put one foot in front of the other. Do you have enough faith to take a single step? What single step could you take today? Affirm: I start where I am and do what I can. Write it out on an index card and read it daily.

"Whatever you can do, or dream you can, begin it.
Boldness has genius, power and magic in it. Begin it now."
— Goethe

Empowering People

*"Love is unconditional commitment
to an imperfect person."*
—Unknown

Cheerleaders are exuberant and electrifying. Their purpose is to ignite that same fire in their audience. Their influence can even determine the win or loss of a game. As a runner who frequently races, I know the importance of having an audience on the sidelines cheering and applauding my efforts. It is a known fact that you count on them to carry you in the final miles. As I pass by them, I often feel motivated enough to sprint to the finish line. We all need personal cheerleaders, or empowering people, in our lives to believe in us and convey that anything is possible. Empowering people accept you as you really are and enhance your best qualities. They see your positive attributes and build on them.

When I was growing up, my parents did the best they knew how to do to meet my needs, but it wasn't always enough. They didn't have enough energy or time for ten children. There just weren't enough of them to go around. My mom not only had the role of a mother; she also managed the farm and was the supervisor for our hired workers and my siblings and me in the fields. My father began working full time in a factory when he was sixteen years old. He continued there until he retired at age 58. He would check in with my mom daily on his lunch hour to see how the farm work was going. When he came home in the evening, he would take over as our manager and supervisor. Overwhelmed with so many children, work, and life, he had little energy left to meet our emotional needs. I couldn't count on them to be my cheerleaders. That wouldn't come until much later.

It wasn't until I was married with children of my own that my mom became more available. She helped me immensely as she offered me some of the encouragement and time I felt I missed out on as a child. For the first fifteen years of my marriage, I had three jobs. I was a mom, an entrepreneur and a student. My mom helped care for the children while I attended college. At the end of the day when I picked up the kids, she always had a pot of soup, a casserole, or a bag of goodies for me to take home. It was her way of supporting me and showering me with her love. I think she overcompensated for the times she neglected me. Over and over she would tell me "Theresa, I am so proud of you for going back to school." Over and over again she told me to call or stop by if I needed her. Over and over again I did just that and thrived on the encouragement and support that I had missed in my early years. Earning my degree wouldn't have been possible without my mom's love and support.

At the same time my dad gave Roger and me two acres of farmland. We used it as collateral to build our first home. Without the land our own home wouldn't have been financially feasible. Even though my emotional needs as a child were often neglected, my parents did the best they knew how to do for me at the time. Later when they had the opportunity to do more they did. Today I know they are there for me, and I count them as supportive and empowering people in my life.

Roger, my spouse of thirty years, has always believed in me. Since the time we met, he saw so much more potential in me than I ever saw in myself. He never doubted me. When we were growing up, my father's idea of a date was for our boyfriends to work in the fields with us. Roger worked by my side for two years. I was seventeen and pregnant with his child when I married him. Four years later we were parents to four little girls. He continually expressed his love for me. When I felt we needed to attend various support groups to help us become better parents, he followed my lead. After ten years of marriage, he agreed to go to counseling with me when I felt that we couldn't go on any longer unless we improved our communication. He cheered me on through college and cried proud tears when I eventually graduated nine and half years later. During the last thirty years, he has supported me emotionally and financially in every business venture I have been involved with.

I remember when I was sixteen years old and he first began telling me that he loved me. I would look at him and say, "Why?" I wasn't used to receiving showers of heartfelt love, and it drove me crazy! My family wasn't affectionate, and I felt very uncomfortable. Eventually I felt safe in his presence as he provided the space that allowed me the courage to be receptive to his love. His heart was on fire with love for me. Little by little I chose to accept it, and as I did his love stoked my own fire and amplified my love for myself. He provided the love, the support and space I needed to learn to love myself. I learned from him that I was worthy of love. Only from my acceptance of his love would I learn how to parent my children in a loving way. He opened up a new way for me to be in the world. He gave me a place to grow my own soul.

Empowering people give you the safe place you need to look into your heart, discover your purpose and follow your dream. Listening to your heart is not easy. Discovering your purpose and passion is a process. It takes work and courage to know who you are and what you want. That's why it is so important to find people who will empower you. Surround yourself with them. Friends often tell Roger and me how lucky we are to have each other. Our relationship isn't about luck. It is about our life long work together. It is about our commitment to love each other and our acceptance of the imperfect. It is about being blessed and receiving those blessings. It is about opening our hearts to our greatness. Our relationship is a gift from God.

"To love somebody is not just a strong feeling—
it is a decision, it is a judgment, it is a promise."
— Erich Fromm

Form Your Dream Team

Four of my girlfriends are all entrepreneurs like me. I feel energized and alive when we are together. It all began at a seminar for beginning speakers. We were advised in a break out session to establish a Dream Team, a group of people who would support, listen, understand and help each other. We would also be required to challenge, confront and push one another to our limits. We began meeting twice a month, opening our meeting with a short period of silence to become centered. One by one we would talk about how the others could support us or what vision we wanted them to hold for us. Then we would pray together. We found that when we parted we left feeling stimulated and ready to take action.

These friends and I share many commonalities. We each have faith and confidence in ourselves and therefore can have faith and confidence in each other. We are comfortable with intimacy and therefore can affirm, praise and speak our truth with one another. We have all climbed mountains, fell and slid down, and climbed back up again. We all believe that we have the responsibility to help make our world a better place. We are committed to doing that.

I was talking on the phone one day telling my friend Barb that I was afraid, "What if I can't do what is required of me? So what if I have the talent, so what if I have the time, so what if I am supposed to do this work. There are times when I am TER-RIFIED!" Barb replied, "Tess, that is your ego. Don't listen. We are on a mission from God. We HAVE to do this work. Fear is not an option." Once again I was invited to live from faith rather than fear. An invitation like that is one of the greatest gifts that empowering people bring each other. This work is my mission in life, and no matter how difficult it is, I have to continue moving forward.

God has big plans for all of us. It is helpful to remember that we are not only working for God but also with God. It is a partnership where we walk hand in hand with God to accomplish our life work. We all have talents, gifts and a mission given to us by God. It is difficult to find happiness in life if you don't use them.

Each person on my dream team is a powerful motivator, balanced with an ability to sit quietly and pray. We spend one weekend a year together. We talk, walk, dream and plan our coming year. We set goals, and we pray for each other's vision and hold it close to our heart. One of the activities we do every year together is to make a vision board. We cut pictures and words out of magazines that have meaning for us; they represent our vision and goals for ourselves. Then we create a collage with the materials we collect. Finally we hang it in a place where it is seen often. The purpose is to use it as a reminder of our dream and to hold our vision clearly in our mind. It is a tool that keeps us focused.

In a creativity class I offer, I have participants make vision boards for themselves. Lucy, a participant in the class, told me about her divorce ten years prior. She believed she was ready for a new relationship and couldn't understand why she hadn't found anybody. I told her I thought she presented herself as a woman who was so well put together that it was possible men didn't know that she was looking for anyone. I then asked her how well she received or asked for help from the opposite sex. Lucy was quiet for a few minutes and said she never looked at it that way. She also said that this made sense.

Lucy included a picture of a man in her collage. Her intention was to be in a new relationship soon. She began paying attention to the way she presented herself when she was with men. She also began a group for singles that met on Friday evenings at the gym. After the workout everyone would go to dinner together. She prayed about her intention and soon found herself dating a man who had joined them for dinner one evening. When you are willing to join your energy with God's, anything is possible.

Because of our relationships, visions, and meetings, there is a bond between the individuals on my dream team. If one of us feels jealous of another, we talk about it. If one of us loses our confidence, we talk about it. If one of us feels another is on the wrong track, we point out what we see. If one of us feels like giving up, the others offer encouragement. We share leads, contacts and resources. We have all agreed that we can advance farther by sharing, helping and connecting instead of competing.

Milton Mayeroff, writes in his book, *On Caring,* "love is the selfless promotion of the growth of the other." When we share our resources, wisdom and love, it multiplies tenfold and returns to us. When we are together and connected, we can feel God's love working through us. Fear and doubt evaporate in an atmosphere of love. Empowering each other leaves us feeling invigorated, stimulated and alive. We have the opportunity to value, trust and love each other as we do our life's work. When that happens the human spirit is heightened to a level of sacredness.

I have been very fortunate to have many such people in my life. It seems as if every decade of my life brings me a new group of friends. What a blessing! I think of them as my soul connections. I believe we find these people when we are ready and open to growth and support. I think new friends and empowering people are always available. The question is, will you take the risk that is required to reach out and invite them into your life?

The risk involves learning how to love on a deeper level. The risk is allowing others to see who you really are and to be open to receiving love and support. If you haven't been able to accept this in the past, it can be difficult. A Dream Team will help you become comfortable. Intimacy is often defined as IN-TO-ME-SEE. When we don't think well of ourselves, we usually want to hide. The risk is to become emotionally naked. If we don't take the risk, we keep ourselves from reaching deep into our hearts and discovering who we are and what gifts we are meant to share.

Sarah Hughes was in fourth place at the winter Olympics games in Salt Lake City when she decided to go out and just have fun in the final competition. Hers was a performance of a lifetime! She did things that hadn't been done before. She not only won the gold medal but, as stated on the front page of a popular magazine the following week, "She took our breath away!" Sarah's smile and glory will never be forgotten. Her family is a big part of her Dream Team. Sarah's father always told her, "The happiest people aren't necessarily the ones with the most good fortune or wealth. They are the ones who share whatever they have with others." Sarah's performance to win the gold was her gift to us.

My friend Karen was a young social worker who had a dream of building a private practice specializing in art therapy. Karen's husband offered the financial support as well as the emotional support she needed to make her dream come true. She also found a mentor who worked as an art therapist. She soon began offering weekend retreats for cancer survivors. As time passed Karen began doing less therapy and more artwork She began working at an art gallery one day a week. Five years later she opened her own gallery where she continues to paint, sell her artwork and offer workshops. The support Karen has from her spouse, mentor and friends continues to empower her today. Karen remains an inspiration in my life as well.

Look around. Who could be your support if you invited them in? Once we become open, God supports us. What holds you back from forming your own Dream Team? What holds you back from gathering the support needed to search your heart and find out who you are and what you have to offer to others? Imagine what life would be like if you did. Imagine a group of like-minded individuals being a phone call or an email away. Imagine beginning Monday mornings with your Dream Team and being affirmed and feeling empowered for the coming week. Imagine walking away from that meeting with a portfolio or briefcase containing the gifts of self confidence, love, and support that in turn can be offered to the co-workers and clients with whom you come in contact. It is a briefcase that offers strength for difficult days.

"Love turns upon a commitment to a certain kind of seeing, a certain kind of sharing."

— Robert C. Soloman

Whom Do You Need to Release?

One way you prevent empowering people from coming into your life is not allowing room for them. Your life may be filled up with too many unhealthy relationships that zap your energy. You know who they are because you leave their presence feel-

ing depleted. You often feel guilty if you do.
zappers your time, energy, and gifts. You are s
their needs, you have no energy left for yourself. .
being responsible for people who won't take responsi
themselves. If you are going to move forward in your h. , it is
necessary to disconnect with energy zappers. You need that
energy to accomplish your own goals and dreams. It is time to
stop being responsible for irresponsible people and get on with
your life.

People change, directions in life change, and often it is necessary to release relationships or friendships that hold you back.
It is a part of life. Often you stay in relationships out of fear.
Successful people help propel you forward, and sometimes that
is too difficult to take. Low energy is easier to handle than fear.
You don't release people from relationships because you are
unloving or uncaring. You release them because their purpose
in your life has been fulfilled. Release them, bless them and
send them on their way. It is a gift to them when you do this.

Likewise when friends move away from you, they are giving you an empty space that will allow others to step in. We
move in and out of others' lives as we grow and evolve. It is our
attachment to others and our attachment to how our lives should
be that causes us pain. When you are open and free, you make
space for empowering people to come into your life and support you on your journey.

"We are each of us angels with only one wing,
and we can only fly by embracing one another."
— Luciano deCrescenzo

Soul Stretching

☆ ☆ ☆ ☆ ☆

1. Fill in the blanks. When I spend time with _____, I feel drained of life energy. When I spend time with _____, I feel alive and I know I am a better person because of his or her company. I know my friendship with _____ isn't good for me. What I need to do in order to release this relationship is _____.

2. List in your journal opportunities that you have missed in life because you didn't allow time for them.

3. How you can further protect yourself from giving away your power to the energy zapper in your life?

4. _____and _____ are two people who are safe to contact and ask for help and support.

5. Choose Your Dream Team: These are people who are on the same journey as you are. You will meet with them regularly, once or twice a month for two hours. The purpose is to give and receive the love and support you will need to fulfill your dreams.

6. Create your vision board: Gather friends and magazines and put your goals and dreams on a poster board. Cut out pictures and words and get creative. When you are finished hang it where you can see and hold a vision for your future. Think big; the sky is not the limit!

7. Who do you know who really cares, tells the truth, supports, defends and loves you?

8. Who do you know who has followed his or her heart and succeeded? Would you be willing to set up an information interview with this person?

9. Do you know someone who could help accelerate your growth and be your business mentor?

10. Identify role models for strength and inspiration. A role model can be a great leader past or present who has achieved excellence or it can be a fictional character. An inspirational role model is someone who can demonstrate what's possible and provide an invaluable source for strength and hope.

---

*"You are a child of the universe, no less than the trees
and the stars; you have the right to be here.
And whether or not it is clear to you, no doubt
the universe is unfolding as it should."*

— Desiderata (Max Ehrmann)

On Higher Ground

"I thank you for this day of life
For feet to walk amidst the trees
For hands to pick flowers from the earth
For a sense of smell to breathe in the
sweet perfumes of nature
For a mind to appreciate and think
about everyday miracles
For a spirit to swell in joy."

— Unknown

What Are You Grateful For?

Years ago in November, I began a family tradition. I reflected on each month of the year, beginning with the previous November, and wrote down all that we as a family had to be grateful for. Then I would read it as a blessing on Thanksgiving Day to my family. What we discovered was that our immense blessings were often hidden in the ordinary experiences and details of our everyday lives.

We found that going together to "Wendy's" after winning or losing a basketball game, and sharing our experiences and feelings of excitement and laughter, or disappointment and tears, was more meaningful than the new CD player under the Christmas tree. Going to Grandma's to bake and decorate sugar cookies, eat popcorn, watch movies, and sleep with her on the sofa bed had more meaning than the biggest and best-wrapped birthday present received. The letters we wrote back and forth when two of the girls were exchange students, one in New Zealand and one in Mexico, lit up our days like the stars lit up our nights. We still have them in a box in the attic. Those were the teenage years when they drove us so crazy that we couldn't wait until they boarded the plane, but once they were gone, our hearts ached for them to be back. That box contains the memories of the precious moments of our lives for those two years.

Now I am in my middle years, and my writings and experiences of gratitude look a little different, but my heart continues to burst with appreciation in the same way. I am grateful for the moments I experience while visiting my aging mom. I hate that she is losing her eyesight and that she has fallen a few times this year. But I love the fact that I am self-employed and can get away for short frequent visits. I savor her soups, her kisses and the touch of her worn and wrinkled hands.

I am not happy that my daughter Shelly and her family moved to Detroit, two and a half hours away. I miss the ability to jump in my car and have her help me with my hair, and I miss the hugs and kisses from my grandchildren. Yet, I am grateful that Kevin found a new job, Mackenzie loves her new school, AJ got a new puppy, and we are all growing from this experience. I miss the two children who live out of state. I can count on one hand how often I see them a year. My friend Kay told me a long time ago that my children are on earth to bring love and light to dark places. I am grateful for airplanes, inexpensive tickets online, long weekends, and the work my daughters have.

When I am challenged with my computer skills, I am grateful my daughters Nicole, Kara, or my friend Rob patiently help me until I GET IT! I am very social, outgoing and active. As a counselor I have to sit for hours. So it is a challenge to spend more time sitting and playing with a computer. I do it because it is the way of the future, and as my children say, "If you snooze you lose, Mom." I do it because life is change and

I must change with life. I am grateful that I have the sense to know and accept change.

I am grateful that I have the sense to ask for help or whatever else it is that I need. If you don't ask for help, you won't get it. In any relationship it is necessary, at some point, to ask for help. If you don't you will end up feeling like a victim. I have found that people want to help me. Roger has always been willing to help me. When the children were young and I was overwhelmed, he helped me with the dishes, the laundry, and meals. He wasn't always happy about doing it, but he was always willing. Now that we are at midlife, he helps me with my business and caring for my aging parents. I have learned to express my gratitude more frequently to him so he knows and feels appreciated.

I have always found it easy to talk with my colleagues when I feel stuck with a client that I am counseling. One of the reasons I have been successful is that I have been willing to say, "I don't know." Rosalyn Baker, a friend and mentor is one of the most understanding and supportive people I know. I never feel inadequate in her presence. Through her, I learned that experts ask for help. Often Rosalyn told me she only uncovered what I already knew.

The fastest way to get what you want is to give others what they want. There are many professional speakers who have been willing to give me guidance. Michael Karpovich tells other speakers to call him anytime after 5 pm. He is also generous with his time after chapter meetings. Bob Danzig and Callie Ottinger have provided my daughter and me opportunities to contribute to their new book. Greg Bauer gives freely of his time and encourages me to keep networking. Barbara Stellard gave me one year of encouragement and direction. Speakers in the National Speakers Association believe in giving back. Barbara Badaloti has given me encouragement for a lifetime. Chuck Cote gave me his phone number and permission to call anytime. For all of these mentors I am grateful. Life is not a competition, and only by helping each other can we all move ahead.

My father always suggested "asking" when we didn't know something. If you can get out of your ego self, help is always available.

I found my first counselor when I was 28 years old. My life was crazy and out of control. I was overwhelmed with the girls and felt as if I couldn't control my anger. Later Roger and I went together to work on communication issues. We also gave our children the opportunity to get help. We didn't have insurance to cover the expense, so we paid out of pocket. The results from our hard work kept our marriage intact.

Now as a counselor, coach, and professional speaker, I have the honor of bringing hope to other people. Phil Berrigan, a priest and activist, spoke of his work with prisoners. He said to watch them grow and transform is like being a "spectator at creation." When clients come in, commit to change and do the work required, they leave different people. I am also blessed to be a "spectator at creation." I take my job of bringing hope to others and offering them a place to heal very seriously. For me there is nothing more important than that, and I am grateful.

One of the most enlightening things that I have learned in life is to be thankful for relationships that challenge me. Prior to learning this I felt like a victim. I felt unfairly treated. I felt I was right and others were wrong. I wanted to run from people who didn't agree with me. Now I know that the people in my life are my teachers. The person in the elevator, the stranger in traffic who doesn't move fast enough, and my co-workers—they are all teachers because they give me opportunities to grow spiritually.

Family and friends are my most important and also my most difficult teachers. They offer me my biggest challenges and opportunities for growth. They show me what character defects I need to work on. Instead of declaring them wrong and heading the other way, I take in what they have to offer. Because of their teaching and my willingness to learn, I have been blessed with opportunities for growth; they are in my life to teach me how to love without conditions. For that I am eternally grateful. It is easy to be grateful for people who don't challenge me. It is wisdom to be grateful for difficult people who do.

Through our culture, movies, and storybooks, we are given an idealistic image of relationships. We have images of what perfect families should look like and we want them for ourselves. We have been taught to believe that greeting cards, glitzy wrapped packages, large houses with picket fences and fine jewelry and dining will bring us happiness. These are wonderful things, but they will only bring temporary happiness. None of these promise love. Relationships provide your biggest challenges and also your greatest opportunities to give and receive love. Strive for healed relationships instead of perfect relationships. When you have loving relationships, you have less desire for the external gifts and thrills our material world offers. Your happiness doesn't depend on the approval of others. Your income or bank account doesn't define your success.

"If the only prayer you say in your whole life is 'thank you,' that would be enough."

— Meister Eckhart

What's in Your Shadow?

In order to heal your relationships and accept people as they are, it is necessary to look at your shadow side. This is your dark side, the part of yourself that you are ashamed of or embarrassed about. It is fear, judgment, perfectionism, control, resentment, regret, guilt and greed. Each of these is part of you and part of me. The reason I can recognize these traits in others is because I have them in me. Instead of denying your shadow side, you can become grateful for it because it allows you to heal and grow your relationships. That is its purpose.

Until you do this work, you will not recognize that you are projecting your issues onto others. Shadow work is very rewarding; but it is also difficult because when we do it we feel we are giving up or losing something. Our ego resists shadow work. Shadow work originated with Carl Jung. He believed that we spend the first 21 years of our life carrying a bag over our shoulder and any time we don't like a certain aspect of ourselves, we put it in the bag instead of looking at it, owning and examining it. Instead we deny, resist and forget that it is even there, that is until we see it in another person.

Anytime you are upset, irritated or at wit's end with someone else, it is really about you. It is about what you carry in your bag. Yes, every single time! You are never finished with this work. In order to have healthy, loving relationships, you must continue to take your shadow parts out of the bag and examine them. That is the only way you can grow.

Due to our strong egos, we often have a difficult time doing this. The picture that comes to mind for me is when I am three years old. My mother has me by the hand and wants to move forward. The tighter she holds my hand, the more I pull down and resist with all my weight. Just as when I was three, sometimes I don't want to move forward. I don't want to see what I need to change in order to grow and move on to higher ground. That little three-year-old child screams, "NO," very loudly and holds back out of fear. That is, until I can't stand it anymore. At this point I have a choice to stay miserable in a relationship, end the relationship or do my own work.

I do my shadow work in the morning after prayer and meditation. My intention is to do a personal inventory in order to become peaceful and happy. I find it necessary to use loving eyes and a compassionate heart with myself. I use my journal to write down similar situations. I write down the names of the people who have been the catalyst for similar feelings. I write down the feelings this brings up in me now. With loving eyes I slowly begin to notice MY pattern. I recognize that the control, anger and negativity that I notice in others are about the control, anger and negativity that I feel or have felt. I recognize it because of my own past experiences with a severe case of angermania, controlitis and negativity syndrome. In other words, the person or situation upsetting me is actually mirroring what I need to heal in myself.

Sandy Scott, a minister now located in the state of New Mexico, defines people who rub us the wrong way as "emery board people." These people are in our lives to smooth our rough edges. She also says that tomorrow we will be doing the same thing for which we judge others today. I tell my clients, "If you spot it, you got it." We all have a shadow side. No one is immune. It is how you survived your difficult childhood. Shadow work is enlightening. It takes your relationships to a new level.

When my four daughters were teenagers, our household was chaotic. One difficult day I was telling my therapist how they were driving me crazy, and I wanted to know what to do about "them." I was dumbfounded when she informed me these were my issues and the chaos wasn't about them, it was about me! My daughters were mirroring everything I experienced as a teen. Watching them was like looking in the mirror at myself. I was wise and brave enough to see the chaos was about my past. I was afraid they wouldn't go to college; I was afraid one of them would get pregnant. I was determined to control their lives so things would go my way.

I also learned that I had no control over what they did with their lives, and my only job was to surrender. I learned that they had a right to make their own mistakes. That is how they would grow. Often as parents we want to save our children from making the same mistakes we did. Finally, I learned that I needed to thank my children for challenging me and giving me the opportunity to heal. They were teaching me how to love without conditions! My inclination was to control them because I couldn't stand to see myself so clearly. After healing those issues, it was gratitude I offered. To be grateful for your shadow side and the people in your life who mirror it for you is wise and rewarding.

One aspect of my shadow is my loud voice. My natural tone is loud. As a child I was called the "loud mouth" in my family. Being the sixth born in a family of ten, I used my loud voice to survive and be heard. In every challenge there is also a gift. As a professional speaker, many complement me on my loud, strong voice. In the past if someone mentioned my voice in an unkind way, I could easily be hurt or shamed because of my struggles as a child. But my loud voice is a part of me. It helped me survive as a child, and it is helping me thrive as an adult. I can own that. I can now be grateful for my voice. I am no longer ashamed of it.

"We are all really mirrors disguised as human beings."
— Unknown

Do You Know the Janitor?

The wonderful thing about mirroring is that when you see the good in somebody else, it is because you have the same good in yourself. We also mirror our positive qualities. I wouldn't be able to see the wisdom in my friends if I wasn't wise myself. I wouldn't be able to recognize the gentleness in my spouse if I wasn't also gentle. I wouldn't be able to see the beauty in my children and the joy in my grandchildren if I also didn't have beauty and joy within. I often deny how wonderful I am. I struggle with accepting love. I need affirmations to remind myself I am deserving of love. It is time we love and accept ourselves.

Often more time is spent with co-workers than with family members. It is easy to blame the other person, to feel unappreciated, unfairly treated or unnoticed at work. Every single time you have an issue at work, ask yourself, what button is being pushed for me in this situation? Who is this person reminding me of? What are they mirroring for me?

I keep a box of affirmation cards on my desk and also a small prayer book because there are times when I need to get myself back on track. At work when issues come up, write about them in your journal. Take the opportunity to examine your lesson. Be grateful for your co-workers. They are in your life to teach you to grow. We have the power to change the energy of our workplace when we are able to foster an attitude of gratitude.

Several years ago, I worked at a rehab center for drug addicts. It was difficult work, and I felt overworked and underpaid. Late one Friday afternoon, I was ready to go home. I was exhausted and wondering where I wanted to go for dinner that night. When the elevator stopped to allow me to leave, the janitor on the night shift entered. I smiled and told him to have a great weekend. I had a twinge of guilt for feeling underpaid. He smiled at me and said, "I plan on it!" And he meant it. I learned about attitude and gratitude that day. To be grateful is a complete change of attitude. I also realized how important a janitor is and how unnoticed and unappreciated they often are. I empowered myself to take those few seconds and make them life transforming.

Did you know that the tiny changes brought about by a butterfly moving its wings in San Francisco have the power to transform the weather condition in Shanghai? In the same way the tiny adjustments you make in your life today can cause enormous results later on. It is called the butterfly effect. What if we found ways to appreciate each other at work? Hold a door open for someone. Share your lunch or offer to help someone who is behind in his or her work. Listening would have a big impact. It is a gift in itself. Gratitude at work creates a deep joy that can make any job easier. Be grateful for the ability and the opportunity to serve others. If this were practiced, the energy or atmosphere in the workplace would change. Honorable work and service would become as important as position and money.

Kathy Mattea's song "Standing In the River Knee Deep and Dying of Thirst" was a real eye-opener for me. Often I feel a sense of lack in my life. One of my core beliefs is that there isn't going to be enough for me. There won't be enough business, friends, or creative ideas. There won't be enough money, fun or time. My parents had the same fears. What parent of ten children wouldn't?

No matter how much work we did on the farm, it wasn't enough. Each year my father would decide to grow more produce than the previous year. Each year we worked harder. We were never finished. We quit because we ran out of bushels and baskets not because we were finished. We quit because there wasn't any more room in the cooler, barn or truck to store the produce, not because we were finished. We stopped working at the end of day because we couldn't see well enough to do anymore in the dusk, not because we were finished. We worked on Sundays, and we worked on holidays. The message I internalized was, I didn't do enough or have enough. We would fall into our beds at night dirty, too tired to even bathe. Then we would begin all over again the next day.

When I recognize that my current sense of lack is coming from childhood, I can feel that fear, release it, and take a few moments to breathe in the abundance that is currently available to me. This centers me. This simple practice never fails to put me back on track and give me peace of mind. With this exercise I gain back the sense of safety and abundance that can never truly be taken from me.

When my spouse or I have a bad day, we often play the "Abundance Game." We sit across from each other in the hot tub and take turns stating our blessings out loud. This little game is magical and works wonders for our relationship. The sun shines in our hearts, our eyes sparkle, and we find ourselves walking through the rest of the day on a higher path. Anyone can play! The only rule we have is that we can't repeat what has already been said. You can play it on walks, in the car and even on the phone! Anytime and anywhere you are. The most important time to play it is when you are feeling down and out. It will immediately lift your spirits!

Who in your life do you need to appreciate more? If you find it difficult to appreciate someone, know that you have a grievance with this person. It is impossible to be grateful and be a victim at the same time. Our hearts do not hold room for both. Which one do you choose to hold onto today, victimization or appreciation? What are you willing to let go of? When we close our hearts because of what someone did to us, we believe we are protecting ourselves. "I am in pain so I will shut this person out." What we don't realize is that it is the very act of shutting down our heart that causes us the pain. It is the act of connecting that will carry us home. It is the act of connecting that causes a heart to be grateful. We cannot walk in gratitude with a closed heart.

If you can drop your expectations and be kind, you will be able to move forward into a peaceful state of mind. A grateful state of mind will give you a deep sense of happiness and increased abundance.

When was the last time you felt that you had everything? When was the last time you were grateful for openness, patience, simplicity, kindness, courage, love and gratitude itself? Choose to focus on these, and they will expand. Choose to share these qualities with others, and your heart will expand. Express gratitude to others. It is a way to walk in the world with a happy heart and a peaceful mind.

Life's Teachers

- Be grateful for the person who cut you off in traffic, it will teach you patience.

- Be grateful for a greedy co-worker, it will teach you to share.

- Be grateful for your troubled teenager, it will teach you compassion.

- Be grateful for your meaningless job, it will lead you to something better.

- Be grateful for your current income, it will teach you to prosper.

- Be grateful when you are sick, it will teach you to appreciate health.

- Be grateful for your abusive parents, it will teach you forgiveness.

- Be grateful for who you are, it will teach you self-love.

- Be grateful for your enemy, it will teach you to love others.

Soul Stretching

★ ★ ★ ★ ★

1. Think about the most difficult times in your life. What did you learn from them? How did you grow from these experiences? Write your answers in your journal. See if you can find insights from your past.

2. Carry a small notebook or list in your palm pilot when you see something, hear something, or experience something that brings gratitude to your heart. Transfer it to your journal at a later time.

3. We often put off important things for when we have enough—enough time, money, friends, or recognition. Have you found yourself saying, when I have enough time I will meditate, I will take my wife out for dinner, I will take the kids to the zoo? When I have enough time, I will do these things. Sit in a quiet place, breathe deep and become centered. Decide what for you is enough money, enough time, enough community, and enough health? What is enough? Write your answers in your journal.

4. What could you do to bring happiness into someone's life? Do it and be grateful for the opportunity.

5. Recall all of your previous places of employment and co-workers. Become grateful for them. Make a list of co-workers you like and respect. After each name write the qualities about each that you admire. Identify times you have seen those qualities in yourself as well.

6. Make a list of co-workers you find irritating. Identify those qualities that annoy you about the person. Now identify a recent time in which you have seen the qualities in yourself.

7. Lack of gratitude can lead to jealousy, low energy, low motivation, self-pity, and a sense of lack. When you experience these feelings, do a gratitude check. What in your life can you feel grateful about?

8. Create a list of the ten things you value the most in life. Spend the day being grateful for these things.

9. Give yourself credit for the opportunities you have had to help others. Then be grateful for these opportunities.

10. Begin each day grateful for another chance to begin again.

"It is more blessed to give than to receive."

— Acts 20:35

You Have Been Given Everything You Need

"Money can't buy love and happiness. In one telephone survey, two hundred and seventy five people in the San Francisco Bay area were asked if they believed that they would be significantly happier and more loving if they had a million dollars. Seventy-six percent of the respondents replied, 'Yes. Absolutely.' Then the Research Company contacted ten millionaires, and asked them, 'Did making your first million dollars make you a happier or more loving person?' The response was unanimous: 'No.'"

— Dan Millman

Do You Have an Attitude of Abundance?

If you live with an abundant attitude, you are a giving and generous person. No matter how much you have, you believe you have enough to share with others. You live life with your mind, heart and hands open. You understand the concept, *to give is to receive.* Your faith is in the abundance of God, and you know that you can't out give God.

When you focus on money alone, you limit your experience of abundance. If you are alive, you are abundant. When my daughter Kara was born premature, she was placed in the neonatal intensive care unit. Everywhere I looked there were tiny sick babies; some weighed less than one pound. When Roger put his hands in the isolete, his middle finger was bigger than Kara's leg. I was very young at the time. I learned what a precious gift life is as I watched Kara for the next month fight for her life. You take health for granted until you watch it slip away from someone you love.

Today's culture cons you into believing you need a bigger everything to be happy: a bigger car, house, business, and bank account. Just as you get a bigger something, you are enticed into getting a bigger something else. The idea that more and bigger is better creates the rat race, a constant competition with your neighbor or co-worker that leaves you feeling anxious and empty. With a continuous feeling of desperation, it becomes impossible to slow down and work on the only thing you do need: a relationship with God. When you have that connection, it allows you to begin to connect with others instead of compete with them. Connecting with others means everybody wins. Competing with others implies someone loses. With God it is impossible to lose.

Last spring I looked into an opportunity to speak at a women's retreat, which was being held at a beautiful resort out of town. I sent in my promotional package and later followed up with a phone call. My intuition told me that I wouldn't be hired for the job. In my heart I knew my friend Rosie could get the job if she knew of the opportunity. I called Rosie, gave her the information and encouraged her to follow up on it. It turned out to be her highest paid speaking job yet, with a promise of a free weekend at the resort for her and her family and a guarantee they would bring her back the following year if they were pleased with her presentation.

The best way to get what you want from life is to help others get what they want and need. If you want more abundance in any form, link your motivation to love and serve others. It is the only way to feel complete, happy and alive. Serving with a loving heart increases your faith that you will always have enough. Open your heart and serve.

"Expect your every need to be met, expect the answer to every problem, expect abundance on every level, and expect to grow spiritually."

— Eileen Caddy

Are You Aware of Your Abundance?

It's important to take time to meditate on and be thankful for all of God's gifts. Recently, I came into work on my day off to find my amaryllis blooming and a money order in the mail from a client whose last two checks bounced. Later, while I was working at my desk, the phone rang twice with clients wanting to make appointments. That evening friends came over, and we welcomed in the New Year!

Often the simple day-to-day abundance I receive goes uncelebrated unless I choose to become consciously aware of it. It is easy to become so focused on the future that you miss the present. It takes focused attention to remain grateful for every-day things such as food, a home, health, friends and family. Winter in Michigan is dreary, and until I become conscious of the snow that sits on the bare tree branches like balls of fluffy white cotton, I fail to see the beauty of winter. I pause a few seconds every morning to notice and give thanks for waking up next to the warm body of my partner. I have been married for thirty years and forget that everyone doesn't have this opportunity.

Life is rich, yet if you don't remain vigilant, you miss the gift of the present only to keep demanding, requiring and desiring more in the future. That is the road to unhappiness. You can increase the quality of your life when you choose awareness. This awareness is a higher level of consciousness, a way of life. If you want to grow, awareness is required to move to the next level.

Abundance is a feeling, a sense of appreciation in this moment, a state of consciousness. Feelings of lack often breed jealousy, greed, and contempt. You can't cheat on your income tax if you come from a feeling of abundance. You can't withhold anything from anyone when you are living in a state of awareness and abundance. The miracle of the loaves and fish is the idea that you have more to give than you know and then some.

Jim was overwhelmed by bills and complained about them constantly. The neighborhood knew just how many bills poor Jim had. He hated paying them so much he procrastinated until they became overdue and it was necessary to also pay the late fee. Then he complained some more. Jim didn't feel worthy of life's gifts and pleasures. He didn't feel he deserved to prosper. He lived his life afraid that he didn't have enough money. Instead of living with an open heart and open hands, his were closed shut, clenched by fear and anxiety.

Amber was a single mom who worked full time. She also had a part time job on weekends doing house cleaning. She brought her two adolescent daughters along to help her. Sometimes she promised them that she would pay them a $15.00 allowance for helping her. Amber would procrastinate paying her daughters the promised amount. When she did finally pay them, it wasn't the amount they were promised. The girls had to wait and often beg for the amount due them. They grew up feeling unworthy and undeserving. These experiences with their mother had a direct effect on the girls' feelings of worthiness as adults. As grown women it was necessary for them to affirm and believe they had a right to prosper; begging and waiting isn't necessary. You are born into an abundant universe. Claim it for yourself. Abundance is your birthright. It is God's good pleasure to give you the kingdom. Learn to live joyously, lovingly, and expectantly! Help others do the same.

What is your greatest giving experience? My daughter Kara is an incredible giver. She teaches art classes to more than nine hundred children in a low-income public school serving primarily the Latin community. Roger and I recently visited her and were amazed at what she had accomplished in a short period of time. She showed us a mural in a nearby park which she and her students had painted. She spent hours of her free time there teaching the importance of beauty. The mural has been there for a year, and it continues to be graffiti free. Then she pointed to where she had the kids plant trees in honor of those who died on September 11, 2001. Different classrooms adopted the trees and continue to nurture them. Kara also started the school's first recycling program. Kara goes above and beyond what is required of her. She is getting married next year and moving to another city, but Kara's work will continue to bless others long after she's gone. In two short years she has left a legacy.

What did you learn from your parents about money? How do you feel about your bills when they arrive? Do you feel ripped off or cheated when the price of electricity increases? Do you resent paying money you owe? If you have scarcity thoughts or negative feelings when your bills arrive, you are blocking the flow of your prosperity.

Have you noticed that when the price of gas goes up, it becomes the hot topic to gripe about? When a gas war is going on in my city, there is a local radio station that will promote a certain gas station offering gas at a ridiculously low price. So many people will drive across town to buy cheap gas, the promotion causes traffic problems. Did you ever notice how crazy we get over a two-cent increase on a gallon of gasoline? We give up our peace of mind over the price of gas, something out of our control. Refuse to complain about the price of gasoline. When I pump my gas, I mentally create a gratitude list. I am thankful not only for the gas but also for my ability to get out of the car and pump it. I bless my car and become grateful for all the safe trips that I have taken. I become grateful for the gas itself for being in such abundance. I pay for my gas and I cheerfully greet and thank the attendant.

Prosperity is a state of mind. It is an attitude to practice. There was a time in my life when I didn't have a reliable car and didn't have the resources to travel as freely as I do today. When my daughter Niki was four years old, she asked me why I didn't wash the brown spots off my car. She didn't understand you can't wash rust off. Giving thanks for everyday luxuries eventually becomes second nature. You do it without even thinking about it. Your thoughts and actions reflect your gratitude. Complain less. Remain open and receptive to receiving more in your life. Serve others with joy. Changing your thoughts will alter your life. It is important to change your thoughts, your focus and your attitude to gratitude as often as necessary. Focus on what you have and move toward what you want.

Susan was in her mid-sixties and lost her partner in a car accident. She felt terrified and believed she was incapable of getting a job to support herself. She was afraid of being homeless, of getting sick, and not being able to make it on her own. I asked her to name all of the people in her life she felt cared for her. Then I asked her if she thought all of these people would allow her to go homeless or starve? Of course, they wouldn't! If any one of them were in her position, would she help them? Of course, she would! Then we talked about other resources she could call upon if she needed to. This simple exercise gave her more security and strength. Those friends, family and resources on her list were a form of abundance in her life. Susan just didn't recognize that fact. In the future, I advised her to think of her list when she became frightened. It helped her to stay focused on the present moment as she looked for suitable employment. She replaced the fear of the future with her plan and the fear of being alone with thoughts of her support system. She reached out and asked for help. She began networking. She called upon each person who offered to help her.

When you lose a partner or spouse, the grieving process can take up to five years. It is important to understand that just when you think you are doing better, another wave of devastation may come over you. Eventually Susan decided to quit her low paying job, sell her house and travel. Through her grieving and loss, she was given the gift of a new found freedom.

Is your faith in giving? Is your faith in health, wealth, and happiness? Do you believe you will get back what you give tenfold? Or is your faith in lack and fear? You cannot feel fear and gratitude at the same time. You cannot feel fear and abundance at the same time. If you feel fear, it could be a wake up call to save more money, to balance your checkbook, or to pay your bills. Listen to your fear. In spite of all his fears about not having enough, my father was always generous with the produce we grew on the farm. He donated fruits and vegetables to the church festivals. If someone at the farmer's market had difficulty paying him, he wouldn't charge him or her. I remember being in the car when he would leave a couple of cantaloupes or a watermelon on a doorstep and quickly pull away before being noticed.

My mother's life is a demonstration of prosperity. She loves to bake and always makes enough to share with others. When we were in high school, she would give us pies, breads, and cakes to bring to a friend's house when we were guests. She spent her life helping and giving freely to others. She never complained about having ten children. She did her best to meet our needs. As we were growing up, she always made room in our home for family, friends and neighbors who needed a meal, a place to stay or a job on the farm. She continues to be a blessing to anyone who comes in contact with her. We were taught young that helping others is life affirming. Today, on a fixed income my mom has a generous spirit that continues to touch the hearts of her thirty-three grandchildren and countless great-grandchildren.

"God gives us two hands, one to receive
joy and happiness and the other to give it away."
— Elizabeth Barrett Browning

What Is Your Dream?

As a young girl, Mother Teresa had a dream to build a mission in India. She began with three pennies. Her superiors in Rome laughed at her, believing she couldn't do much with three cents. The tiny nun who stood only four feet eight inches tall told them, "With three pennies and God I can do anything."

Mother Teresa was spiritually generous; she did difficult work with the filthiest people in the dirtiest places. Her intention was to serve God, and she did it with great love. She connected to the poor through God's love. Retirement was not in Mother Teresa's plan. She worked until the end of her life, building 517 orphanages, homes for the poor, AIDS hospices and charity centers in one hundred countries. She did it with three pennies and God.

Begin today to move toward your dream, toward doing your work on earth. It is necessary that we all live up to our potential. No one can do the work that you came on earth to do. Do not compare yourself to others. Do not wait until you have enough money. Pursue your dream with your heart and soul. The only thing necessary is a connection to God. You will be led from there.

I became pregnant when I was seventeen years old, a senior in high school. My boyfriend of two years, Roger, was three years older than I. At the time our country was involved in the Vietnam War. He left for boot camp three days after we were married. When he slipped that thirty-five dollar ring on my finger, he had a one-dollar bill in his back pocket. We never thought about how we were going to make ends meet. We were too young and naïve to care. Our only plan was love. Within four years we were the parents of four beautiful daughters. The odds of our marriage surviving were slim, but we never gave up. At times we couldn't do much more than put one foot in front of the other. So that is what we did.

We were never afraid of not making it financially. We had a connection with God and faith in a vision that all would be well. When money was scarce, we worked two or three jobs at a time. After thirteen years of living on the family farm, we moved to the city. We wanted a new beginning for ourselves and for our children. We discovered that East Grand Rapids High School was ranked among the top 10 high schools in the country. We also heard that more than ninety percent of the graduates finished college. We dreamed that our children would do things we didn't do. We wanted to give them an opportunity to dream the same things for themselves. East Grand Rapids sounded like the place for our children. We never questioned whether we could afford to live in that neighborhood. We moved in with the attitude that we would be an asset to the community, and we were. That move gave our children opportunities that weren't available in the country.

Upon graduation Shelly attended a private business college. Nicole spent her senior year in high school as an exchange student in New Zealand then enrolled at Michigan State. Kara went to Mazatlan, Mexico, as an exchange student and then enrolled at DePaul University. Kristy graduated from East in the top ten of her class. She was also voted "female athlete of the year." Her dream was to play sports at a collegiate level, and she chose the University of Chicago.

Kristy was born without most of her right hand, including her fingers. Throughout her life Kristy was determined to be like other kids. In order to be accepted she needed to do what the others did. When her sisters began playing sports, she wanted to play as well. She played softball, soccer and basketball. There were times her stub would be cracked and bleeding. She played anyway. Roger put up a basketball hoop and paved our driveway. He spent hours challenging her to be better and play harder. She spent her free time endlessly shooting hoops and going to summer camps. She constantly challenged guys to play one on one with her. She would go to the park and find a way to get in the games there. She never gave up. We couldn't either.

We didn't know the cost of tuition at the University of Chicago. We never checked it out. Kristy told us that she wanted to play basketball there because it was a Division III school, and she felt she would have a better chance to play. Besides being Division III, it is known as one the best schools in the country. So we sent a video of Kristy playing to the women's basketball coach at U of C. A few months later, she called us for an appointment. Sitting in her office, I picked up a brochure that stated tuition was twenty-nine thousand a year. I passed the brochure to Kristy and Roger, and at the same time, I mouthed the price behind the coach's back.

We were dumbfounded, "clueless," as my kids would put it. Often times I get so excited about life that I just forge ahead without gathering all of the information. I never even inquired about the cost of tuition there. Therefore, we never let the idea of the cost prevent Kristy from applying. As we stood in the coach's office, she told us they were reviewing Kristy's case in the financial aid department as we spoke. She told us to come back in four hours for their decision.

We walked around the campus silently. What could we say? "Kristy, you can't go here. We can't afford it." We already promised her twin sister that she could attend DePaul and tuition there was fourteen thousand per year. I prayed silently as we walked. I asked for guidance. I asked for a sign that we were doing the right thing, that this was the right school for Kristy. I needed to know that we were on the right path. As we strolled the campus, I continued to pray for a sign. Our belief in Kristy kept us going; we were also inspired by her. Her dream was to play ball at a college level. We were not about to give up now.

One of the fun things about being so young and raising four daughters so close in age was that we had a lot of the same interests. We liked the same activities, sports, movies, and music. Even though I was their mom, I could relate well on other levels. For example, Kristy and I were both runners, and we listened to upbeat music when we ran. We learned to roller blade and entered races together. The year she graduated from high school, a group of musicians called "Ace of Base" were popular. As we walked back to the coach's office, a small sports car with its sunroof open and radio playing passed by us. The song that came to my ears was "I saw a sign" by Ace of Base. At that moment, as crazy as it might seem, I knew we were in the right place! I thought of it as synchronicity. In a matter of minutes, the coach informed us that Kristy would receive a grant that would cover three quarters of her tuition. We looked at the situation not only as affordable but also as a miracle!

When you worry about expenses or about how unfair life is and doubt what is possible, you become stuck. Life becomes limited. Victimhood limits your vision of what life could be. Abundance is a state of mind. Prosperity is a choice. Just as we chose East Grand Rapids, we were now choosing the University of Chicago. Again we wanted the best for our children and weren't willing to settle for anything less. I was determined our children would have the education that I had missed out on at their age. During her junior year, Kristy had three different part time jobs to help pay for her living expenses. She played soccer and basketball for two years. She loved the excitement of traveling every week with her teammates to other cities. This opened up a new world for Kristy. It not only strengthened her faith but the faith of our family that with God anything is possible. When a mountain seems too high, the only choice is to scale it and keep the faith!

"So much has been given to me, I have not time to ponder over that which has been denied."

— Helen Keller

Soul Stretching

★ ★ ★ ★ ★

1. Practice tithing. For many people tithing, or giving 10% of their income, sounds like too big of a step. Begin giving whatever you can. If you are a two-income family, give 10% from one. When you feel comfortable begin giving from the other as well. Tithing will draw more abundance to you. Tithing is a test of faith. You can't out give God.

2. Strengthen your relationship with God. Focus on serving others. Focus on what you can give instead of what you want to receive. Sit quietly and ask yourself, "What can I do today that demonstrates all my needs are met?" Some suggestions:

- Smile at everyone you meet.
- Take a friend to lunch.
- Visit a sick or elderly person.
- Buy somebody a bouquet of flowers.
- Volunteer to help out with children.
- Count your blessings.
- Dream big.
- Plan a vacation and set a date to take it.
- Send a check to your favorite charity.
- Take time to help someone.

3. Make a prayer box. When you find prayers or words that inspire you, put them in a special box. I often tear out the page in my "Daily Word" if it is especially touching. I also save prayers that are given or sent to me. I save them in my

box, and when I experience difficult times and doubts, I reread them. I have been doing this for five years and have collected an assortment. It takes me a couple of hours to go through the entire box. I always feel blessed when I am finished.

4. Go within and ask for guidance. Sit quietly for ten minutes. Ask what you need to do and where you need to go. Write down the answers you receive. Then begin.

5. Pay your bills and taxes on time. Bless and thank the people and places that have served you.

6. Do one brave act today. Do it with love and for a good purpose.

7. Today live life with joy and enthusiasm.

8. Volunteer to help someone this week.

9. Share your talents with someone.

10. Donate to a charity.

"I thank You God for this amazing day:
for the leaping greenly spirits of trees and
a blue true dream of sky; and for everything
which is natural which is infinite which is yes."

— e. e. cummings

Love the One You're With

"To be nobody but myself—in a world which is doing its best, night and day, to make you everybody else—means to fight the hardest battle which any human being can fight, and never stop fighting."

— e. e. cummings

What Are Your Core Beliefs?

I believe one of the most difficult lessons we have to learn in our lifetime is how to love ourselves. We constantly want to change everyone else when all we need to do is love ourselves. We continually want to possess people, status, money and things. We only need to fill our own heart with self-love.

If you weren't properly cared for and nurtured as a child, it is important to re-parent yourself, to give yourself the love and care you continue to need. Within each of us is a small child wanting to be held, nourished, comforted, and loved. How will you respond? Once we begin to allow time for loving ourselves, obtaining anything else is simple because we believe that we are worthy and deserving of it. I will be with me for the rest of my life. You will be with you for the rest of your life. So learn to love the one you're with!

The first step is becoming aware of what you think about yourself. Do you continue to put faith in the core beliefs you learned as a child? One of my biggest core beliefs was, "I am unfairly treated." The truth is that as an adult I can't be unfairly treated unless I allow it. The question is, do I treat myself unfairly in any way? If I don't get enough sleep, exercise, healthy food or meditation and prayer time, I am treating myself unfairly. If I don't walk my talk, if I don't love my body, if I don't respect myself, I am treating myself unfairly. If I don't embrace myself with love, I am treating myself unfairly. What would it take to love yourself? What would you need to change?

To discover how you betray yourself, ask the question: "What are my bad habits?" These habits become addictive and seductive. They are life sucking. Sitting in front of the television, a couple of glasses of wine with dinner, spending more than you make, gossip—these are all examples of bad habits that can spiral out of control. They will fill you with self-hate rather than self-love. They will keep you stuck and feeling lifeless. Anytime you find yourself lacking energy, look at your habits. Are they helping you or hurting you? It is as simple as that. Anyone can change. Do you have the willingness and desire? Are you ready to do the work?

When we are children, we don't have much power to control the way we are treated by parents, teachers, siblings or neighbors, but as adults, we do have that power. We teach others how to treat us. If you allow someone to disrespect your boundaries, you are responsible for the mistreatment. If you allow someone to take advantage of you, you are responsible. If you allow your energy to be depleted by another's presence, you are responsible. You are responsible for the way you allow yourself to be treated. You choose what to believe about yourself, how you treat yourself and how others treat you. If something isn't good for you, don't allow it into your life.

"Everyone has in him something precious that is in no one else."
— Martin Buber

Can You Love Yourself Enough to Change?

When I was a teenager, I began smoking. I was rebelling. No one could stop me from doing it. When I smoked I also felt that I fit in with my peer group. Smoking gave me a false sense of power. Later as a parent I kept my addiction hidden from my young children. I didn't want them to smoke when they grew up. I was always sneaking around wondering when and where I could smoke my next cigarette. I smoked when they took their naps, and I smoked after I put them in bed for the evening. One day I was smoking in the bathroom with the window open. My daughter Nicole knocked on the closed door and stated in her sweet little voice, "Mommy, I smell something in there." That was the day I knew I couldn't hide it anymore. On November 17th, 1983, National Smoke Out Day, I decided to quit smoking. That day I made a commitment to my health. I loved myself enough to change my life.

I knew that in order to be successful I had to replace smoking with something else. We had a family friend who was a runner and that always looked appealing to me. I began running on an indoor track at the local college. When I began, I walked more than I ran. I added a lap every week; my goal was to add an additional mile every month. The following spring on a sunny spring day in April, I ran outside for the first time. I was up to five miles! I began running in the evenings, one hour after our family finished eating dinner together. I would lace up my shoes and hit the road feeling free. It became my alone time and Roger's time with the children. Strength and courage allowed me to take control of my life. Running gave me time to clear my head; it kept me sane.

Grand Haven always has a road race on Memorial Day Weekend. It is 10k, or 6.2 miles, a "kick off to summer run." On race day I registered and found my place behind the starting line while my family found a place on the sidelines to cheer. I was the last runner to cross the finish line.

I continued running after we ate dinner as a family and found that if I ate meat my stomach would become irritated. I quit eating meat. After six months of watching the races from the sidelines, Roger decided to quit smoking. He also began running and entering races with me. We often put our kids in the fun runs, which were a mile long. Every finisher would get a ribbon. We found ourselves going to road races all over the state. My daughter Kristy soon began entering the longer runs. Today five of us continue to run. Kristy has run two marathons; Nicole has run a half marathon and is in sales for an athletic shoe company. Roger and I have run together for the last nineteen years. Our family has learned that to be happy we need to be healthy.

Decisions are easy when you know what your values are, when you know what path you want to take. My decision to quit smoking was like a pebble that created a ripple effect in my family. I had no idea how it would affect our lives. When you take a stand for loving yourself, those around you can't help but do the same. Loving yourself is necessary for a happy life. Loving yourself is necessary if you want others to love you.

"It is only in adventure that some people succeed in knowing themselves—in finding themselves."

— Andre Gide

Are You Good Enough?

Another core belief of mine is, "I am not good enough." Many if not all of you have been told this by someone: a parent, a teacher, or even a coach. You believed it then, and you continue to believe it now. Our thoughts are seeds we plant in the garden of our minds. If we water and fertilize our negative core beliefs that were planted in our childhood, we will be rewarded with more like-minded negative beliefs and thoughts. It's like crab grass. When you try to pull it out of the ground, some of the roots always break off, and it grows back. If you allow negative thoughts and core beliefs to continue, they will spread and seep into every area in your life until all loving thoughts are choked out. Stuck in your life-draining habits, you will harvest low self-esteem, self- sabotaging behavior, and self-hatred. To take a stand for love and demand respect is an act of courage that will change your life forever.

Any physical, emotional, verbal, or sexual abuse you received as a child from your caretakers helped form your current belief system. Unless you change your core beliefs about yourself, you will continue to have low self-esteem as an adult. You will attract others to you who have the same beliefs. It is helpful to spend some time alone, look within, and journal the thoughts and feelings that come up for you and cause you problems. It is a choice to heal your past. It is a choice to let go of fear and do the necessary work that leads to self-love.

When I become stuck and old patterns surface, I watch for painful thoughts, emotions, and attitudes. I write down the event that upsets me, the belief I hold about it, my attitude about the event and my response. For example, an event (Jane forgot my birthday) my belief (Jane is treating me unfairly) my attitude (I will get even) my response (anger and sadness). The truth is Jane meant no harm, but she touched on my old wounds of abandonment. After journaling I am able to recognize that my old beliefs and patterns have surfaced again. My response to myself is, "Oh that's the old stuff coming up again. I don't buy into it anymore." Your old patterns are like reruns; you become tired of watching them. You are an imperfect human being. In spite of that fact, you are worthy, you matter, and you are deserving of love.

> *"Learn what you are and be such."*
> — Pindar

What Seeds Are You Planting?

Sue told me that I have high expectations of my friends. I expect my friends to pay attention to me. I want to be told that I am important; I want to be sent cards and email. I want my friends to call and visit me. I want to know they are thinking of me. There is nothing wrong with these desires. Who doesn't want to receive expressions of love? I feel joy when I receive these things. But my expectations cause problems.

I get myself into trouble when I expect my friends to fulfill my needs as I define them. Love doesn't require anything. I have learned to examine how much time and love I am giving myself when I become demanding of my friends. When I take responsibility for my own needs, I don't rely on my friends to fulfill them. When I honor and love myself, I don't require anything from my friends. I no longer feel lack and no longer project my behavior on to them. I have learned to hold my own hand. Sometimes I feel as if I have a mountain to conquer. The mountain is myself.

If you want to be successful, always bring your problems and conflicts with someone else back to yourself and look within. Ask, what do I think deep within myself most of the time? Then you can discover what unloving thoughts you are sowing. This requires two qualities that are difficult for most of us: self-reflection and patience. Both are ingredients for a wonderful life.

96

Examine what seeds or beliefs you plant daily in the garden of your mind. Each seed represents a thought. Seeds germinate before they sprout. I remember when I was a child, my mom would put vegetable seeds in between sheets of wet newspaper. Then she would place the newspaper in a dark, warm spot. After a few days, she opened the newspaper, and life had sprouted everywhere. When planted in rich soil, the tiny seedlings had a head start. Your self-love will also take time to germinate. Warm your positive thoughts with love and hold them close to your heart while they germinate. Once the new thoughts sprout, plant them deep in your consciousness. They will come into full bloom and multiply. They will be accessible when you find yourself resorting to addictive behavior. Be prepared to reap a bountiful harvest of self-love.

Only when we love and accept ourselves can we learn to love and accept others.

"We should all just smell well and enjoy ourselves more."

— Cary Grant

The Time to Heal Is Now

After several years living on the family farm, I discovered that there wasn't enough physical distance between my new home and family and my old home and family. Our relationships had become enmeshed. There were too many arguments and not enough boundaries between us. When I saw myself repeating unhealthy patterns, I knew we would eventually need to move. I needed to create space and distance between us in order to restore out relationships to health. Making that decision was difficult but also a turning point in self-love and respect.

The move gave Roger and me the opportunity to release old patterns and break new ground. It takes courage to know to take a stand and move on with your life.

We established a new life that included new boundaries, rituals and privacy with our children. It is your responsibility to find a way to heal your past. Only then will you be able to function wisely, to love and work and connect with yourself and all of life. When we built our first home twenty-six years ago, we planted six, small, beautiful pine trees in front. Each tree represented one of us. Today they stand tall; they have grown over the years just as we have grown.

Healing family-of-origin issues takes time. I have tools to rely on when I am tempted to fall back. I am not perfect and never will be. It takes four to five generations to change family history. I continue to do my inner work and have passed the baton on to my grown daughters. Our only lesson is to love each other, love without conditions. It isn't easy. I will work on this until the day I die. I don't think we are ever finished.

Loving yourself requires forgiving yourself. I learned that after I moved. Only after I forgave myself, could I forgive my parents and siblings for any grievances I had with them. Forgiveness isn't a one-time thing. It is necessary to forgive ourselves daily and extend that forgiveness to others. Forgiveness is a way of life. It is the only way to inner peace.

Forgiveness is the water or life force that will make a garden lush and beautiful. Forgiveness keeps your inner garden growing. When we forgive our past and anyone including ourselves who has hurt us, we provide the space to harvest love, respect, and healthy relationships. When your new thoughts about yourself are firmly planted in the garden of your mind and watered every day, nothing can prevent them from blooming. When we take the responsibility needed to change our belief system and become a master gardener, germinating seeds of healthy thoughts, our harvest will be a garden blooming with self-love.

"No one can make you feel inferior without your consent."
— Eleanor Roosevelt

Soul Stretching

☆ ☆ ☆ ☆ ☆

1. It is possible to love ourselves the way we wish someone else would love us. Begin your self- reflection and create your own story of love, one-step at a time. Make a list of things that you can do for yourself that would bring more happiness in your life.

2. Create your own affirmations. Use "I" statements, make them positive and in the present tense. Take time every day to write them, say them out loud, and visualize them.

    For example:
        "I am a beautiful person deserving of love."
        "I am loved and respected by others and myself."

3. Think of someone who irritates you. Write down the things that you dislike about this person. Ask yourself, how do I do these things myself? If the quality you write is judgment, begin to notice how you also judge others. Then affirm, "I release my need to judge others and myself." Be vigilant for these times and repeat your affirmations as needed.

4. Make a list of all the things that hurt you, that caused you to feel pain, distrust and fear. Now write a letter to your parents or whoever raised you. Tell them they are forgiven. Decide to make forgiveness a way of life. Study the following poem.

Decide to Forgive

For resentment is negative
Resentment is poisonous
Resentment diminishes
And devours the self.

Be the first to forgive,
To smile and to take the first step,
And you will see happiness bloom
On the face of your human
Brother or sister.
Be always the first
Do not wait for others to forgive
For by forgiving
You become the master of fate
The fashioner of life
The doer of miracles.
To forgive is the highest,
most beautiful form of love.
In return you will receive
untold peace and happiness.

— Robert Muller

5. Do you need to forgive yourself? Make a list of any mistakes you hold against yourself. Remind yourself that you have been forgiven when old issues surface. Be gentle with yourself. Learn from your mistakes. Do one nice thing for yourself today.

6. Quiet your mind. Identify any frustration, anger, depression or pain that you may feel today. Look for the thought behind the feeling. Change your thought. Tell yourself, "Today is a new day!"

7. Ask yourself the following questions and journal your answers:

Do I judge others?
Do I judge myself?
Do I condemn others?
Do I condemn myself?

8. Notice how you deprive yourself of pleasure. Begin to take the same care of yourself as you would a newborn baby.

9. Too often we try to get our emotional needs met with material things. Love yourself enough to give yourself the following:

    Stillness – Find a quiet place where you can get in touch and listen to what is in your heart. It will calm your mind and touch your soul.

    Faith – What do you believe in? Have faith in positive outcomes. Put your faith in the power of prayer and peace on earth. Faith is sacred, holy and not to be taken lightly.

    Kindness – Get a massage, sip a cup of tea, use the best oils and perfume. Treat yourself as you treat your best friend.

    Comfort – Do you hurt? Are you frightened? Allow yourself to feel your pain. Cry, scream, or journal. Ask for support.

    Relax – Slow down and take a nap, go to bed early or kick off your shoes and listen to your favorite music.

    Peace – Take a break from listening to CNN or reading about war in the newspaper. Instead pray for peace, think peaceful thoughts and express gratitude for your life.

10. Write a love letter to yourself. Thank yourself for how far you have come in life, what you have learned, accomplished and overcome. Put it away for a couple of months, and then mail it to yourself.

"It isn't until you come to a spiritual understanding of who you are...that you can begin to take control."

— Oprah Winfrey

A Bit of Parenting Wisdom

"Love conquers all."
— Virgil

What Lessons Are You Teaching Your Children?

I believe that being a parent is the most difficult job in the world; there is no higher calling. It is a job to be taken seriously. The example we set has the impact of a lifetime. We have a responsibility to help our children become the people they need to be to live their visions. Our children are miracles and the everyday events—dinners, conversations, chores, watching television, and carpooling—are teaching moments, sacred moments. These moments provide fertile ground for children to grow their roots and wings. In these moments you will find opportunities to make the world a better place.

I wish I could go back in time for this. Growing up I never felt smart enough or good enough. I didn't love or value myself so I didn't know how to teach my children to love and value themselves. When my children were growing up, I was still comparing myself to others. So I compared them to others as well. I didn't know that we are each irreplaceable, unique, spiritual beings. We are loving and deserving exactly as we are. We don't need to improve one hair on our heads to be worthy! We all have individual gifts that are a unique part of the puzzle.

Revel in your child's uniqueness. Celebrate each child's greatness. I believe this lesson is the most difficult of all to teach and to learn. Self-love and acceptance is a lifetime process and journey. In order to teach it, you must live it. Allow your children to be who they are, not who you want them to be or who you were. Let their beauty and value touch your heart.

I found my own lessons in my children's errors. I had two big fears for my children. They were based on my own past. I feared they would marry young, and I feared they would become pregnant. I was determined that they wouldn't make the same mistakes that I did. I actually believed that I had the power to do this. I really thought that I could control or change it. I didn't know then that it takes four or five generations to change family patterns. We can only carry the baton so far, and then we have to pass it on to our children. They in turn give it to our grandchildren. That's how family systems change. One generation at a time and only if the desire and work is passed on.

Shelly met Kevin at a teen dance club, "Top Of The Rock," when she was 16 years old. He was older and more experienced than she was. He worked at a local pizza parlor. The first time I greeted him at the door I sensed his desire for her. I wanted to slam the door shut and make him go away. But I couldn't do it. That was not the person I was. He dated Shelly for a year or so, and as we watched the relationship grow, we had no idea how much we would also be growing.

My 17 year-old daughter, a senior in high school, left home on a stormy summer day. I made no attempt to stop her. I knew I couldn't. There was no talking, no touching and no longer any desire to try to work out conflict. Life had become unbearable for us. I had begun to feel like an intruder in my own house.

I wanted to sleep on weekends without waiting for doors to bang shut—a sign that she was safe, alive and unmugged. I wanted to wake up to birds chirping. I wanted to enjoy my morning coffee quietly. I was tired of her blaring music piercing my ears first thing in the morning. I was tired of my sweaters being missing or tossed on the floor. I wanted to listen to classical music, Bach and Anne Murray. I didn't want to wonder what was going on behind her bedroom door.

I didn't like being shut out and disconnected. I was tired of feeling alienated and wounded. I was tired of soggy Kleenex, endless therapy sessions and my obsessive thinking of her. I was tired of silence and glares during the dinner hour and of her untouched food. It wasn't really the food she was rejecting. It felt as if anything I touched was contaminated, and she withdrew from it. I was constantly being rejected. She had a new boyfriend, and I had too many rules.

When she was unhappy, I was unhappy. I thanked God when she packed and left. Her girlfriend picked her up. They put her mattress in the trunk of her blue Chevy. No good-byes, no I-love-you's and no promises to visit were uttered.

But then there was an eerie silence in our house. It was quiet on Fridays, Saturdays, and in the mornings. A plate was missing at the table where she used to sit, and unanswered questions ran through my mind: *What is she eating for dinner tonight—where and with whom?*

A strange emptiness crept in after my daughter left. My sweaters were back in my drawer, her shoes weren't tossed on the rug in the kitchen, and her hair wasn't all over my bathroom sink. But in spite of my work and the freedom I now had to listen to my own music and live my own life, I felt a foolish unstable grief. After all, I had grown accustomed to her troubling me.

After Shelly left, we began talking on the phone, and we listened better than we had in months—even years. I didn't interrupt, and I didn't give advice. I began to savor her visits and phone calls. I put a picture of her on my nightstand next to my bed. And every night before I closed my eyes, I whispered in the dark, "Good night, Shelly, I love you."

Love came through for us. Two years after she left, I became a grandmother, and it has been one of the most delightful experiences of my life. Thank God my daughter and son-in-law (that aforementioned boyfriend) visit with the children often. We have bikes stored in our garage waiting for those little cherubs to bring them to life. Their grandfather has bought them heart-shaped sunglasses to wear when we go get ice cream cones in his convertible. They are ecstatic just to fill the plastic pool with water. Water, doggies and Popsicles are just a few of the simple pleasures that elate them. I am in absolute awe of the blessings this family has bestowed upon me.

Sometimes they sleep over on weekends, and we wake up to the birds chirping. They eat all their favorite foods while I sip my coffee. My grandson dances to Barney and hops to Tigger, and my granddaughter likes to read and paint. When I am with them, I am engulfed with the joy-filled wonder of a child.

On Sundays they come for dinner after church. Amidst the spilled juice and picky eaters sit their proud parents and grandparents in an atmosphere of love. We discuss what words my grandson has learned and my granddaughter's artwork and swimming lessons. Sometimes they sing us songs and tell us stories. I enjoy the fun and laughter that being with them brings.

My daughter continues to call me during the week. We discuss our work, recipes, her sisters and friends. We take pleasure in each other's laughter. We attend concerts together and enjoy the same music and books. Thank God, she calls. She is vivacious, intelligent, and compassionate and has a zest for life. I have pictures of her and her family all over my house, and every day I look at them and smile! It is true. Love does conquer all.

"Smile at each other; smile at your wife, smile at your husband, smile at your children, smile at each other— it doesn't matter who it is—and that will help you to grow up in greater love for each other."

— Mother Theresa

Teach Your Children to Support Each Other

When our children played sports, they were expected to attend each other's games. Sometimes the final scores were close, the cheering was deafeningly loud, the bleachers were packed and everyone had such a good time, we were left voiceless from screaming and cheering. We often celebrated a win by eating at McDonald's or getting ice cream cones. Other times when one of them "sat the bench," the games were frustrating and energy draining and their siblings were uninterested. These weren't fun times, but our family learned that it was important to be there in good times and bad. Supporting one another can be fun and easy and also hard work and difficult. It can mean talking and advising or listening and honoring.

We taught them to take an interest in each other. They helped one another with homework and other projects. When one had to collect bugs for science class, she took her younger sisters with her. When it was their turn to collect bugs, they brought their older sisters with them. Niki ran for class secretary in her sixth grade. She was new to the school and shy. Her plan was to become better known. Her sisters helped decorate and hang posters for the competition. When she lost they helped her take the posters down which enabled them to be available emotionally for her. In spite of the defeat we were supportive of the girls. And afterwards Niki's classmates were more familiar with who she was.

As a child my mom always made a big deal out of our birthdays. Twelve family members meant twelve celebrations. They were the events of the year. She loved to bake a variety of pastries and would allow us to choose what we wanted on our day. We were allowed to invite one friend from school who was welcome to spend the night. There was an abundance of balloons, games, and excitement but nothing compared to the love my mother put into these events.

I continued the tradition of making birthdays a big deal with my children. Kristy and Kara, the twins, always celebrated their parties together. There were twice as many kids, games, and gifts. It was exhausting but fun. One year for Niki's birthday, I made her an 'Annie' doll that was three feet tall. She had a head full of red hair, the classic red dress with the white collar and black shoes she wore when she danced with Daddy Warbucks. I also stitched her dog Sandy as well. I would sew after putting the girls in bed for the night. It was the only way to keep the gifts a surprise. The sewing room was directly above Niki's bedroom. Later Niki told me that she could hear me sewing and would drift off to sleep wondering what I was making for her.

The year I turned thirty Shelly, my oldest daughter, was twelve. She asked her dad for my address book. She wanted to give me a surprise party. She took her plan to her grandmother and together they schemed, giggled and baked. She had Roger take me away while the guests arrived. When we returned my family and friends greeted me with a shout of "surprise." There were balloons and a big sign made by the kids. It was quite a feat for a twelve-year-old, one that I will never forget. The tradition my mother began more than sixty years earlier helped us find joy in celebrating and honoring each other. It is a tradition we continue today.

Teach your children to be kind to each other and to look out for each other. We always told the girls that friends come and go, but sisters are for life. We taught them that teasing, name-calling and put-downs were hurtful and disrespectful. On the other hand, when they were in conflict with each other, we would encourage them to work the problems out themselves and wouldn't interfere unless they were being physical. If they were physical we separated them. Name-calling and put-downs are forms of verbal abuse. They are very destructive. Loving-kindness promotes health and high self-esteem.

As parents, we can expect to make mistakes. You can keep mistakes to a minimum by attending parenting classes and getting a mentor or a therapist. When you parent you learn as you proceed. You often don't see the mistakes you make until the damage is done. Don't expect to be a perfect parent. There is no such thing. Every parent makes mistakes because every parent is human. If you have regrets, apologize to your children, even if they are adults. An apology validates their feelings. Allow your children their point of view. Your children, no matter what their age, want to be validated. If your children are grown, it is never too late to apologize and tell them if you knew better you would have done better. You did the best you knew how to do at the time. Tell them how much you love them every chance you get.

"Trust in the Lord with all thine heart, and lean not unto thine own understanding. In all thy ways acknowledge Him, and He shall direct thy paths."

— Prov. 3:5-6

Rely on the Power of Prayer

Prayer is a very effective form of support. We taught our children to pray together. The year my sister Cheryl was pregnant with her second child, we prayed daily after we said grace, that she would have a baby girl on my birthday. Alexis is 15 now, and she was born on March 5, my birthday. We prayed my mother through breast cancer. We prayed for the soldiers in the Gulf War, we prayed for world peace. We prayed for one girl to make the softball team, we prayed that another would win a basketball game. But mostly we prayed for guidance to do the right thing.

Our children's relationships often mimic our own. I discovered my children were more likely to fight with each other when their parents were fighting. When my children got along, it was because their parents were getting along with each other. When parents love and support each other, the children learn to do the same.

Loving support is the best gift you can give to your children. Often when they are in trouble or take a difficult path, we want to react with anger and blame. When Niki was twenty years old, she dropped out of college after one semester to be with her boyfriend Max. They moved to Florida where they worked in a popular restaurant waiting tables. After several months, she called one night to tell us she was pregnant. She informed us that she and Max were breaking up and her intention was to "plan adoption" for her baby. At this time in her life, she didn't feel she was capable of raising a baby. She asked us if she could come home and live until the delivery. We knew her request would require unconditional love and support. We knew it wouldn't be an easy thing to go through.

We had been celebrating our freedom. We had just brought Kristy and Kara to Chicago to begin college. After twenty-three years of marriage and raising four daughters, we were finally alone. We were still young, and we had big plans. I had just started my internship. We wanted to travel. We bought new furniture. We thought we were in heaven. We felt as if we were beginning our lives all over again. The night the phone rang we were celebrating and toasting our freedom. Then I answered the telephone. After listening to her story, I took a deep breath and told her to call me back in twenty-four hours. I didn't want to say anything I would regret later.

I was in shock. I was angry. I wanted to hang up the phone and pretend the conversation never happened. I wanted to say "I told you so," but I didn't. I felt the freedom I had just gained slipping out of my fingertips and I couldn't stop it.

Growing up, Niki was the child who never gave us any trouble. She was quiet, charming, intelligent, and charismatic. She earned good grades, she was involved in sports, she had a lot of friends and she was funny. In our wildest dreams, we couldn't have imagined this happening. After two days of giving the situation thought and prayer, her father and I welcomed her back with open arms. We told her she could come home to live during the pregnancy and that we loved her and believed we could get through anything together. The only condition we had was that she continue working during the pregnancy. I went back to my therapist to receive support and work through my anger and my guilt for not taking care of the baby myself.

We helped Niki decide what adoption agency to choose. I went to her doctor's appointments and Lamaze classes with her. I helped shop for maternity clothes. When we told our friends about the pregnancy, three couples came forward and told us they wanted to adopt her baby. We were shocked and amazed. We referred them to Niki. This would be her decision; it was her baby. One couple, friends from church whom we had known for the about two years brought over their profile. Niki thought it strange to have people we know adopt her baby. She promised them to give it some thought.

Roger and I liked the idea of our friends Sam and Jane adopting our granddaughter. They told us that we could remain friends, and they wanted us to take an active role as grandparents. Sam and Jane were in their late thirties just a couple of years younger than we were. They didn't have any children, and we trusted them to be good parents.

On New Year's Eve, our friends called and asked for a decision. They wanted to make their plan for the New Year and wanted to know if it should include a baby. That sunny Saturday afternoon, I handed Niki the telephone, and she told our friends Jane and Sam that they could include her baby in their plans for the New Year. Niki had one condition, that they allow Max, the birth father to be involved in the baby's life. They agreed. We took Niki out for lunch and celebrated her decision. Her due date was the first of June.

The closer Niki came to giving birth, the more doubts and opinions our family and some friends had about it working. They were afraid Niki would change her mind at the last minute. They felt we were "giving away family." Our family also thought of us as irresponsible. They believed Niki's job was to raise her child. They also didn't believe we could remain friends with Sam and Jane after they adopted our grandchild. How dare we … and who did we think we were anyway?

Looking back who knows what buttons we were pushing for our friends and family. We felt sad and angry that we didn't get support from my family. We learned to ignore them and let it go. Our intention was to continue with our plan, to allow two loving friends to adopt our grandchild. She deserved to have a wonderful life! We believed they were capable of giving it to her.

I asked my good friend Judy if she would give Jane and Niki a baby shower. We invited our supportive friends. Niki, now seven months pregnant, sat next to Jane and together they opened the baby gifts. Sam, the adoptive father, was so excited he came to video tape the activities. My gift was an album I put together of my favorite pictures of Niki growing up. I wrote stories next to each photo. Tears streamed down my face the entire time I worked on it. The shower was bittersweet; my daughters and I had mixed emotions, we cried tears of both sadness and joy.

We thought of Sam and Jane as additional family. They wanted Roger and me to be active grandparents. They wanted my granddaughter Mackenzie to know her new cousin. They wanted my other three daughters to be active aunts. Their wish was for Niki to be involved as well but respected her decision not to be. Sam, Jane, and Niki picked out the name Ariel together after discovering the baby was a girl. They gave her our last name, Marshall, for her middle name. We thought Ariel was blessed to have twice as many people in her life to love her.

Then when Niki was eight months pregnant, the birth father, Max, unexpectedly came back into the picture. He drove from Florida, knocked on our door one Sunday night and told Niki he changed his mind and now wanted to father the baby. Max's father left his mother when he was a small child. He didn't want to make that same mistake. In a split second, he threw the plan into chaos. Niki didn't believe Max was capable of parenting Ariel either.

Max was young, single and worked as a cook, but he did not want to abandon his baby. He hired a lawyer and decided to settle the matter in court. In the end if Max wanted the baby, he had the right. He was the birth father. We knew in court we would lose. Sam and Jane were devastated and shocked. They hired a lawyer. Niki was angry. As much as my mind was made up, I was willing to surrender. I was out running one day and had a vision of all of us with our hands outstretched to heaven, holding the baby up. My thought with the vision was—God, you decide who will parent Ariel. "Thy will be done."

Niki and I were together in the birthing room while Max and the chosen parents waited outside the door. When Ariel was discharged she would be put in foster care until the judge decided who would parent her. There was a court date set for July.

Ariel was born beautiful and healthy on May 31st, 1995, perfect in every way. She looked like an angel. After the delivery Niki chose Sam and Jane to be the first to hold and bathe Ariel. After they bathed her and dressed her Roger and I each held her. It was nerve wracking and gut wrenching to see Max stand by and only be allowed to observe through the window outside of the nursery. My heart went out to him and I told him so. We supported Niki to the end believing Ariel was meant for Sam and Jane. As difficult as it was to watch Max, we continued with our plan. Eventually Max and Niki were left alone to hold and spend time with Ariel. It was time for Niki to say goodbye. Her job as the birth mother was coming to an end.

When Ariel left the hospital, she was placed in foster care for two months while we waited for the court date to arrive. That was one of the most difficult things we had to watch happen. Max was allowed to visit her once a week. The rest of us had unlimited visits. It was a very difficult time; we felt as if we were in limbo. We were experiencing loss, and we were sad.

Only a couple of my friends continued to support us. One evening my friend Connie came over and dropped off a red jacket as a gift. She told me it was a magic coat meant to cheer me up. It did. She also gave Niki a basket filled with nail polish, cute socks and hair products. Another time when I went to work, my friend Paula dropped by and took Niki out for pizza. It was a quiet and lonely time.

A few days before the court date arrived, the telephone rang. It was Max's lawyer. He wanted to inform us that Max had changed his mind. He would no longer fight Niki's decision of adoption. He decided he was too young to be a father, and it would be too difficult to do alone. At the same time Max made it clear that he would be involved in Ariel's life. Niki had Sam and Jane's promise that they would allow Max to do so. He would be known as Uncle Max. He also requested that he and Niki pick up Ariel from foster care and deliver her to Sam and Jane's house themselves. It was too difficult for Niki to go to the door. She remained in the car. I have a picture Sam took of Max carrying Ariel up the sidewalk to their home. It is the picture of our miracle.

Niki's choices that year changed our lives forever. We were stretched to love, surrender, and forgive on a new level. She gave us an opportunity to practice our faith, values, and commitment as a family. When parents offer love and support to their children during a crisis, they teach the meaning of a circle of love. In a circle of love, miracles happen.

When children know they can count on their parents to support them, they learn to support each other. Siblings who don't learn how to support each other and become friends when they are growing up take little if any interest in each other when they become adults. The girls are grown now, and two live out of state. But we are together as a family to celebrate the holidays, and every Fourth of July we gather at our cottage. We also connect online and cell-to-cell. The girls continue to take an interest in each other's lives. They want to know about their nieces and nephew. They want to know about each other's work. Niki is in sales for a popular athletic shoe company, and everyone in the family wears that brand of shoes. We wouldn't think of wearing any other brand. Our children visit each other, shop together, play together, help write resumes together, and pray for each other. Their lives aren't perfect, but when a conflict arises, they have the wisdom and the support of each other to work it out. They are sisters who have become life-long friends.

"You are a child of the universe, No less than the trees and the stars; you have a right to be here. And whether or not it is clear to you, no doubt the universe is unfolding as it should."

— Desiderata

Teach Them to Appreciate Nature

When we had our flower business, together we planted, harvested, and sold flowers from our two-acre plot of land in back of our home. It was very successful in many ways. The girls knew the feeling of dirt under their fingernails and between their toes. They built a fort in the woods and made tents out of clothesline and blankets. They knew the importance of rain and sunshine. Their innate sense of wonder blossomed on the farm. Where there is wonder, there is spirituality. Being in nature allowed them to see the connectedness of all living things. The beauty of the flowers, the cycles, and the seasons held a timeless connection for them.

The business was very profitable and enabled us to partake in activities and allowed us to take vacations that we wouldn't have had without it. The difficulty for them was that I gave them too much work and responsibility. My expectations were too high. If they weren't in the garden working, they were at an art fair or farmer's market selling the bouquets and arrangements we designed. There were many times they cried and we fought because they didn't want to do the work. Sometimes it was too much to expect from them, and other times they wanted to do something else. I couldn't see that at the time. I forced them to work anyway.

One day I recognized the parenting mistakes I was making. I saw that I was too demanding, that I was expecting them to work as if they were ten years older than they were. Within a year after my new awareness, we sold our house and moved into the city. We never looked back.

When I forgave myself for my own inadequate parenting, I could also see the rewards that my children received. They know the simple pleasure of building forts in the woods and playing 'red rover' and 'red light, green light.' They know the sound of a breeze swishing through sheer curtains on a summer afternoon. They have memories of picking and eating the first raspberries of summer. They know the smell of clean sheets dried on the clothesline. These are blessings of country folk who grow up in relationship with nature.

When they were growing up, we ate dinner every night—the weather permitting—on the picnic table. It was a table Roger built, and when we moved we brought it with us and used it in the city. It is more work to carry everything outside and in again after eating, but the rewards are enormous. Some of my favorite memories are when we were sitting around the picnic table eating dinner. It was a simple pleasure that put magic in the ordinary. It is one of many soulful memories of life on the farm.

Besides a love for nature the biggest asset the girls gained from our flower business outdoors is their work ethic. They know the blessing of doing good and honorable work. They are self-sufficient adults doing their part in making our world a better place to live. They continue to love and spend time in nature.

"Life is better when it's fun. Boy, that's deep isn't it?"
— Kevin Costner

Teach Them Responsibility, Respect and
How to Love Unconditionally

Give your children choices. They will learn responsibility. Often times we want to make decisions for them. We don't want them to make the same mistakes we did in our past. Our ego takes control, and we tell them what they should and should not do. If you take choices away from your children, they will be dependent on you. When given choices they develop their wings to fly.

Give children consequences. If they break something, they need to replace it. If they want something, teach that it is possible to earn it. My children received gifts when it was a holiday, a birthday, or a date that had significance. They appreciated what they received. It is sad to see the senseless junk that fast food restaurants pass out as toys that are in the trash or left on the floor of a car minutes after they are received. Disney makes billions on toys that are important until the next blockbuster appears. Children are flooded with temptation as our cultural values scream at them from cereal boxes to underwear. Parents spend money they don't have believing that the products will buy the kids at least temporary happiness.

I believe it was a blessing that because we didn't have much money, we often had to say "no." Many times parents give in because they want to be liked by their children. Love your children enough to allow them to hate you. It feels as if they hate you when you tell them "no." They might be mad for a few minutes, hours and if they're teenagers even days. But they will get over it. They need parents not friends.

My daughter Kristy was born without fingers on a very deformed right hand. I quickly realized that if I did things for her, she would never be a responsible adult. She learned how to tie her shoes, hold on to her bottle and a swing. When she was six years old, she learned how to wash and dry dishes. When she complained and cried that she wanted sympathy, we offered encouragement instead. We required that she do her part like everyone else in the family. I used to tell her it might take her a little longer than her sisters to get her work finished but she was fully capable. We didn't make excuses for her. By the time she was eleven years old she was the pitcher on her softball team. She played soccer and basketball in high school and for two years at The University of Chicago. She was able to do this for one reason. Our family held her accountable. She learned responsibility.

When our girls complained about not having everything everybody else did, we took them to "God's Kitchen" where we signed up to volunteer preparing and serving food for the homeless. They were struck by how much some people didn't have. They learned how to care for strangers and support people who had less than they had. They learned we not only had enough of everything for ourselves, but we had enough to share. When children learn to help and support each other, they learn how to extend it outward to those around them.

The only children who will respect others are those who respect themselves. Consideration of others is becoming a lost art in America. We push and shove our way to be first and get our share any time there is a limit on something. We hate to wait in line, be stuck, or slow down in traffic. Profanity, nudity, violence and rage are the norm in entertainment. When courtesy and consideration are taught at home, it can be extended outside the home. Teach your children how to take turns, use manners, and respect the elderly and people who are different from themselves. Children mimic adults. Check your own behavior. Improve your patience. Send blessings and love to cashiers, operators, and others in service work. Teach your children to do the same.

Unconditional love is the most difficult lesson of all. Often when our children are in trouble or causing trouble it becomes difficult to love them. Love them anyway. Never threaten to take your love from them. Promise that you will always be there for them and you will always help them no matter what. The only gift we have to offer them that is worthwhile is our love. Even Anne Frank at twelve years old continued to believe in the good of all humans. Guns and other weapons help people feel powerful. If they felt loved, they would know that no other power is needed.

Our children are vulnerable, tender and in dire need of guidance about what makes life meaningful. Trust your intuition and hunches on what your children need. No one can be a better parent to your child than you. When you make mistakes, forgive yourself, learn, lighten up and move on. Miracles come from taking action. Each moment presents a new opportunity to begin again.

God's plan for your family is bigger and better than your plan. Do your best and learn to surrender what you can't handle. God will take care of the details. Remember to give yourself sacred times for renewal and energizing. Seek uplifting books, friends, ceremony, ritual, nature, private time, and prayer. By remaining alert to the amazing wonder in you and in life, you can make each day a new beginning!

"Experience is a hard teacher, because she gives the test first, the lessons afterward."
— Vernon Saunder's Law

Soul Stretching

★ ★ ★ ★ ★

1. Show your children how to find beauty everywhere: in color, movement, music, words, sounds, textures and fragrances.

2. Encourage imagination. Introduce your children to new ideas and role models. Take them to concerts, dances, plays, art fairs and museums.

3. Make magic out the ordinary. Monitor the use of television, computers, and games. Allow time for arts and crafts. Have an indoor picnic. Eat dinner in the morning and breakfast in the evening.

4. Teach the gratitude attitude. Keep a thanksgiving journal on the kitchen counter ready and available for entries throughout the day.

5. Establish a ritual of daily quiet time. A half hour before bedtime will quiet down the entire household and keep peace.

6. Be a positive mirror for your children. You teach by example, everything you do or say will teach your child something about the world and where they fit in.

7. Demonstrate responsibility and refuse to blame others. You are responsible for your attitude, your tone of voice, your self-care, and your life. Your children will learn this from you.

8. Teach commitment. Do what you say you are going to do. Tell the truth and keep your promises.

9. Pray and remind your children to pray in the midst of big and little struggles. It will help everyone release worry and anxiety on a daily basis.

10. Teach your family to exercise and eat healthy foods. These two things done on a regular basis will affect everything else you do.

"How do you say, 'I love you?' Often, and loud!"

— Leo Buscaglia

Conclusion

"Commitment brings peace of mind;
not the end of the journey, but the end of wandering;
not the end of a road, but the end of searching for one."
— Leslie Weatherhead

L ife is a journey from birth to death. Flying by the seat of your soul lifts you higher than your doubts and your problems. Fly joyfully and expectantly. The trip is too short to be a victim. Sometimes you don't have control over what happens on your flight but you always have a choice as to how you react to what happens. The attitude you choose to travel with will determine the flight pattern.

Christopher Reeve is my personal hero. In spite of losing his most basic freedom—the freedom to move—he continues to juggle his acting and directing careers, political activism, his foundation and his role as a husband and father. He does this while undergoing intense physical therapy to maintain his health. Christopher has a vision. He knows who he is and what he wants. He has an "in spite of" attitude. He is committed to thinking, seeing, and acting with a *yes* regardless of his challenges. Christopher may not be able to move, but he can fly. He has flown above paralysis, doubt, and fear. He uses prayer, trust, and a positive attitude for fuel.

How are you traveling through life? Choose to be a high flyer. From time to time, your family, friends, coworkers, neighbors, or boss may be seated next to you. There have been many times when you have hurt and disappointed each other. Love yourself and the people in your travels in spite of vivid memories of unlovable times. Let go of what they did, and what you did, and the meaning you have given it. Release blame and resentment. It isn't possible to take this trip without being hurt and disappointed by people. It is part of being human. Accept this fact. Make peace with your enemies. Fly above the battlefield and gain a new perspective. Drama is too heavy a cargo to carry. Love and learn from each person you come in contact with on your journey. Thrive on cooperation. Keep your word. Learn compassion, forgiveness and patience. These will allow for a safe landing in emergency situations.

Live an undivided life. Be yourself no matter where you are or what you are doing. Live an authentic life. Stand up for what you believe in. Be passionate about your work but don't let it consume you. Remember when the journey is finished, you will leave your trophies behind. So allow time for breaking out of efficient, goal-directed and bottom-line thinking. Express a caring attitude, and discover the joy of service.

Lighten up and make time to reflect on where you are and where you are going. Notice the scenery. Appreciate the trees, flowers and animals. Breathe. Dance. Celebrate. Reflect on where your journey is taking you, what you are doing and with whom you are doing it. Enjoy your surroundings, the sights and the smells. Remember with God as your pilot, your real purpose is to give and receive love. Recommit to your purpose and continue flying each day as if is the final day of the journey!

"My life was a risk—and I took it!"
— Robert Frost

About the Author

Tess Marshall is an expert on helping others reinvigorate their lives and work with joy and meaning. She has dedicated her life to teaching people how to be outrageously happy at home and at work. As an inspirational speaker, she has the ability to connect with an audience and blend wisdom, stories and humor in a unique and inspiring way. Drawing on her experience as a therapist, she is able to guide and prepare people, intellectually, emotionally and spiritually for change in their personal and professional lives. Tess is available to speak for corporate retreats, conferences, and meetings.

If you have a story about transforming your work and life and would like to share it, please send it to Tess Marshall's e-mail address: TessMarshall@TessMarshall.com. You are invited to visit her website where you will find more information on her credentials, range of clients, and the topics on which she speaks.

www.TessMarshall.com

www.flyingbytheseatofmysoul.com

Check it out because life's too short to be unhappy!